a Guide to Reading the Old Testament

Part One

God Begins

Revised Edition

ACTA Foundation
4848 N. Clark St.
Chicago, Illinois 60640

NIHIL OBSTAT
Thomas B. McDonough

IMPRIMATUR
✠ Joseph Cardinal Bernardin
Archbishop of Chicago
September 25, 1985

Published by ACTA
4848 N. Clark St.
Chicago, Illinois 60640
(312) 271-1030

Library of Congress Catalogue No. 85-70360
ISBN No. 0-914070-21-5

Printed in the United States of America

INTRODUCTION

At one time or other most of us have felt the terrible depression of loneliness. Perhaps, we were traveling and arrived late at night in a strange town. The station was practically deserted and the few people around us wore the indifferent expressions of strangers. We were all alone.

After the creation of Adam and Eve, God could have left human beings to their own devices, especially when we think of the shabby way they had treated their creator. But God has never abandoned them. He was and is so deeply concerned for men and women that he himself became human, suffered, died, and rose again to restore all people to his friendship.

In a very special way the Gospels tell us of God's concern for us. This is why they are called Gospels, which means "good news." But, in one sense, we might call the whole Bible a "gospel", for there is one message that stands out on its pages; it is God's deep involvement in human history. So we are never really alone. God is with us and speaks to us.

In the words of Sacred Scripture we find God's message to his children, his words of advice, his assurances of love, but most of all, his plans for our future. His message to us has taken many forms, so as to be appealing to all people in every circumstance and time. But though he speaks in a countless variety of ways, it is of Christ he speaks.

"In times past, God spoke in fragmentary and varied ways to our fathers through the prophets; in this, the final age, he has spoken to us through his Son." (Epistle to the Hebrews, ch. 1:1).

Christ is with us in the Blessed Sacrament of his love.

Christ is with us in his Mystical Body, the Church, whose members we are.

Christ is with us in the words of the Bible.

Not everything he says is easy for us to understand. But we must not let a difficult phrase or a puzzling event deprive us of this life-giving contact with Christ. The important thing is *to read*. To read *often* and *regularly*. Little by little, the pieces will fall into place, and we shall see the great plan of God for our happiness centered in Christ and his Church stand out clearly against the background of changing times and events. We will become increasingly aware that his word to us is no dead letter, but a ringing challenge. We have a part to play in his plan for our happiness.

God speaks to us; but it does not end there. He expects an answer. This answer is prayer, not only the prayer of heart and mind, but also the prayer of action. The prayer of a life lived out in carrying forward the wonderful plan of God for human beings, here and now in our own generation.

There are many ways of reading the Bible. We might start at the beginning and read straight on through. We might pick it up and read it at random. A third way is to follow a sort of basic reading plan. For in order to get the full impact of what God is saying to us, to find in the Bible that meeting-ground with Christ, it is necessary to have some understanding of the great sweep of events and ideas. Where is it all heading? Why did this event take place? How did this man further God's plan?

These guides follow the third way. They give a basic reading plan of the Bible. They are designed to help you get the broad outlines of God's activity in human history. They hit the high spots — the great turning points in the development of the plan. The four booklets in this series cover the whole sweep of the Bible from the first book to the last. However, they are designed to be only a jumping-off place. After you have gone through the material and read the selections from the Bible, you will be better prepared to strike out on your own, and by further reading, fill in the plan sketched out in these booklets.

This is the first book in the *Guide to Reading the Bible* series. The eight lessons in this booklet trace the development of God's plan from its beginning with Abraham, some 2000 years before the birth of Christ, up to the time of the Northern Secession, 1000 years later. This, the first great set-back of God's work, divided the people of God into two hostile factions, North and South.

After most of the lessons, short essays have been added. Some of these essays, called BACKGROUND, provide the information necessary to understand the text. Others, called MARCHING ON, will carry forward the history of the people of God.

A word of sincere thanks —
- to Daniel Lupton, who wrote the original manuscript,
- to Irwin St. John Tucker, who inspired and encouraged the idea of such a reader's aid.
- to Russell Barta and Vaille Scott, who provided a way to field test this approach,
- to Fathers John F. McConnell, M.M., and John P. O'Connell, who read the text and made valuable suggestions, and finally,
- to Fathers Edward Mehok and Gerard P. Weber, who revised this text.

The four books in this series

(Available in English and in Spanish)

A GUIDE TO READING THE OLD TESTAMENT
   PART ONE: GOD BEGINS
   PART TWO: THE STAGE IS SET

A GUIDE TO READING THE NEW TESTAMENT
   PART ONE: THE MYSTERY OF JESUS
   PART TWO: THE WHOLE CHRIST

ACTA (ADULT CATECHETICAL TEACHING AIDS) is a not-for-profit organization. Its purpose is to assist in the teaching of the Catholic Faith through the preparation of materials, such as texts, films, and recordings.

Sources of the Jordan at the foot of Hermon
6 ft. above sea level
Over a distance of 10 miles the Jordan drops 700 ft.
The coastline south of Carmel is straight. Only at Jaffa is there a kind of natural harbor; Herod made use of the reefs in the building of Caesarea
OMRI builds a new fortified capital on the mountain of Shemer, with good communications to the coast and the trading centers of Phoenicia
Lower than Judea, with many fertile valleys
Jaffa to Jerusalem a distance of 39 miles by road
Widest section of the Jordan valley, 12 miles across
Fertile plateaux parallel to the central ridge and called the 'Lowland' (Shephelah) in the Bible
the Kingdoms of Juda and Israel
Fertile coastal plain becoming narrower to the north
South of this peninsula the water is only a few feet deep
Beer-Sheba to Dan 196 miles by road; 150 as the crow flies
Mt. Hermon
Tyre
Dan
UPPER GALILEE
Lake Hule
Sea of Galilee
GALILEE
CARMEL
PLAIN OF ESDRAELON
ISRAEL
Gilboa
Samaria
Shechem
VALLEY OF THE JORDAN
PLAIN OF SHARON
MOUNTAINS OF SAMARIA
Jaffa
Bethel
Jericho
Jerusalem
PHILISTIA
MOUNTAINS OF JUDAEA
Dead Sea
JUDA
Beer-Sheba
NEGEB

CONTENTS

LESSON 1

St. Paul in chains

The Plan of God . . . An Overall View

In your study of the Bible you will discover something very important. In some ways the Bible is not one book, but a whole library. Many authors have contributed to it. Men varying in background from common laborers to sheltered scholars and mighty kings. The Bible took more than a thousand years to reach the form in which we know it. At first glance it is an apparent hodge-podge of history, scraps of battle songs, poems, family trees, legal codes, plays, short stories, prophecies, political speeches and sermons, to mention a few of its elements.

But the important thing you will discover is this one startling fact. Throughout the whole work there is one unifying thread which draws the whole thing together. The Bible is the story of God's activity in human history. From the dawn of time God has been working out a plan to bring the human race to salvation. A little corner of the Near East was the workshop in which God was to hammer out people's salvation by preparing them for the coming of Christ and his Church.

God reveals: God revealed himself to us, not suddenly or completely — for, as the Bible tells us, "Who can see God and live?" Rather, step by step, a little at a time, as his people were ready for it. "In times past, God spoke in fragmentary and varied ways to our fathers through the prophets."—HEBREWS ch.1, v.1.

Our task: It will be our task to trace this gradually developing communion with God through the record given us in the pages of the Bible.

Where do we start? Begin with the last pages of the Bible. With St. Paul. Why here instead of the first pages? Well, if you would really understand an acorn, you must first get a good look at the finished product, an oak tree. So also, if you would understand the full message of the Bible, you must not begin with the first faint outlines of God's Plan, but with its full development as found in the concluding pages of the Bible. So . . .

NOW OPEN YOUR BIBLE AND READ:

ST. PAUL'S EPISTLE TO THE EPHESIANS
Chapters 1 through 4

(You may also wish to read the story of St. Paul's adventures in Ephesus. You will find it in the Acts of the Apostles, ch.19 and ch.20. It will take you only a few minutes to read but is important to catch what St. Paul is saying "between the lines".)

behind the words

The people of Ephesus were especially close to St. Paul. Their city figures prominently in the story of the Acts of the Apostles. St. Paul had good reason to remember Ephesus, for he was almost the victim of a lynch-mob there and narrowly escaped with his life. The Christians of Ephesus, like their leader, had been subjected to violent persecution. The town itself was an important center of trade and learning. It boasted a famous shrine to the goddess Diana and did a brisk business in souvenir statues of the goddess. St. Paul

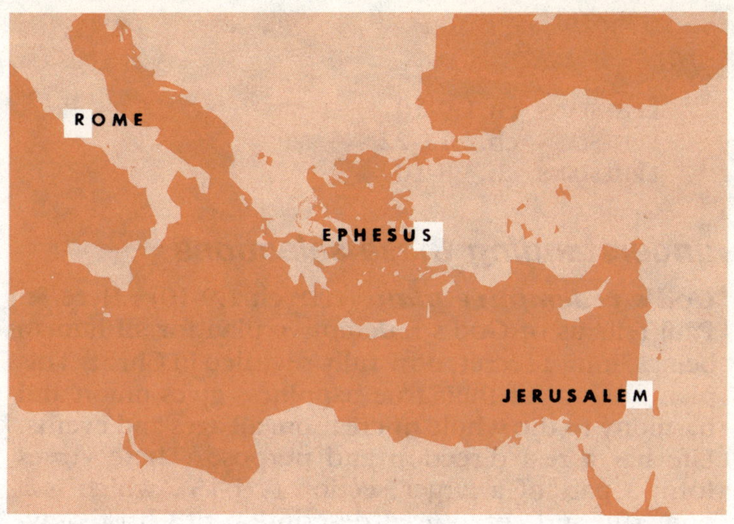

spent two years in Ephesus, and wrote this letter back to Ephesus during his imprisonment at Rome.

Considering the close bonds of love and friendship which united Paul and the Ephesians you may be surprised at the markedly impersonal tone of this letter: it points up the whole purpose of God's activity in human history culminating in the Incarnation of Christ and extended and continued in his Church. Surely, such an important message was destined for the widest possible circulation, so it had to be couched in general terms.

It may well have been sent to the Ephesians first, because of the old and enduring friendship of the Apostle, but no doubt copies were quickly made and dispatched to the other neighboring communities.

One of the best ways to make the basic message of a book one's own is to mark the key passages. This can be done by underlining, checking, marking with a see-through colored pen, or writing in the margins. In the course of our lessons, we will point out some key passages for marking.

> EPHESIANS, ch.1:9-10
> EPHESIANS, ch.2:11-22
> EPHESIANS, ch.3:8-10

understanding these selections

God's redemptive plan: (EPH. ch.1:9-10)   Here St. Paul tells us of God's redemptive plan for all human beings, long a secret, now fully revealed in Christ. This plan of God for their true happiness gives union and harmony to the whole of creation, all ages and events. Life has a real direction and purpose. These verses form a part of a larger section (v.1-15), which is a powerful and enraptured description of Christ's saving work. It has been called a 'Hymn of our Redemption.''

All are called: (EPH. ch.2:11-22)   This is, in a way, the key passage of the whole letter. All people are now called to the life-giving intimacy of God's family. All people are now the inheritors of those ancient promises of God to a single nation, the Jews. We must try to imagine what wonderful "good news" this was to the Pagan world of St. Paul's day. Often the greatest philosophers of the time could find little or no meaning to life, and certainly the cruel life of slavery, the lot of so many members of the empire, offered little to make life joyous. But now men and women were to learn that life was important, that they were important. They were not mere cogs in a machine but members of the household and family of God.

Christ and his Church: (EPH. ch.3:8-10)   In this passage St. Paul speaks of the solidarity between Christ and his Church. The Church continues Christ's work on earth. The Church, open now to all, is the extension and presence of Christ down through the ages to the end of the time. Christ is with us through his Church still carrying forward God's great plan for our salvation.

point of these selections from Ephesians

Here the Apostle tells us what the Bible is all about. It is the record of God's efforts to prepare people for the Church of which we are members. All that happened in past ages when this plan was developing is not far off and strange to us. Our roots go back through the centuries.

We are there with Moses on the Mount of Revelation; we are there with David at the beginning of the Ark of the Covenant to Jerusalem; we are there beneath the Cross; we are there at the Ascension; we are there at the coming of the Holy Spirit. For we are members of the people of God and nothing has happened, or will happen, to his people which is foreign to us.

bible and church

Throughout literature "the journey" is a prominent motif. This journey may consist merely in a number of stops along the way. Nothing may be happening in the minds, hearts and souls of the characters. They may only be pieces of baggage being carried on a train of events. Or the journey may be a story of an interior search for meaning, a true pilgrimage, a continuing struggle to change and grow spiritually.

The Church has just such an exciting story of a people's interior search for God going back almost four thousand years. The first two thousand years of this story is recorded in Scripture. The names and places may seem strange to us, as they certainly were to the Ephesians and to the other Gentile converts, but Paul invites us to see them as our ancestors in salvation history, our family in faith. We may be separated from these people and events by thousands of years and thousands of miles, but what we are reading is the saga of human beings learning about their God and themselves, both as individuals and as a community.

We read and retell these family stories of our spiritual heritage not merely for the historical facts or for the entertainment they provide, but for the lessons we can learn about who we are, where we hope to go and how we might get there.

This story of the Church, of the People of God, of those who are "one in Jesus Christ", is not yet completed. It is still being played out in the life of the Church. It continues in our individual lives. We are still writing it. It is like a tremendously large painting called "The Church" which is being painted by many different artists. In the center stands the triumphant Jesus. As we look at the canvas we see that some sections are finished, others are just begun, and some are blank. Some sections are beautiful and some are ugly. As yet we do not see the complete and overall plan for the painting. But each of us has a tiny brush and the paint of our lives. To fill in the section given to us we need to know what has happened in the past; we need to understand all that prepared for the coming of Christ so that we can grasp what has happened since he came and where we fit into the picture as individuals and as the Church of the twentieth century.

doers of the word

"Act on this word. If all you do is listen to it, you are deceiving yourselves."

JAMES ch. 1:22

The study of the Bible will be a meeting with God if we undertake it with faith and prayer.

It is helpful to set a time aside each day when you will not be disturbed to read the Bible. Read a chapter or two each day from the book presented in the lesson. Quietly reflect on what God is saying to you. At times you will hear nothing. That is alright. At other times, he may speak loudly to you.

The Church has always had the highest respect and deepest love for God's written Word. She uses it in every Mass to carry his message to us. As it is proclaimed by the reader we should concentrate on what the words mean in our lives and on what we hear God saying to us individually at this time in our lives.

questions

(The questions are designed as a self-test. If you are able to answer them, you will be fairly certain that you have mastered the main points of this lesson. The answers are contained in the material you have just read.)

1. Why is it a good idea to begin your study of the Bible with a reading from St. Paul instead of beginning with the book of Genesis?

2. What is God's plan for humankind?

3. What is the Bible all about?

4. What is the most profitable way for you to study the Bible?

topics for discussion

"Where two or three are gathered in my name, there am I in their midst"

MATTHEW ch. 18:20

(These questions are designed for use in groups who are studying the Bible. A cooperative sharing of the results of reading and study can greatly enrich the individual's own understanding of the Word of God. These questions can also be used by an individual reader to help him or her reflect on the message the passages have for himself or herself.)

1. What do you hope to get from studying the Bible?

2. In your own words how would you express what it means to you to be a Christian?

3. In the first three chapters of the Letter to the Ephesians what does St. Paul say about what it means to be a Christian?

4. What experiences have you had which have helped you see God's plan for you working out in your life?

BACKGROUND:

The making of the Old Testament

The Bible resting on your table as you're reading these words was not handed to Moses by an angel of the Lord. There are many years of history lying behind that book. Remember that God's Word was in the first instance, a spoken one. St. Paul tells us that faith comes by hearing. Our Lord, himself, commissioned the apostles to preach, not write books.

Throughout the long history of the people of God, the Word of God took many forms of expression. In those days it was a living, not a written word. It might be contained in the tales told 'round the campfire in the desert. It might find a home in the impassioned oratory of a prophet. It might shine through the minute provisions of a written legal code. It might leap from the victory song of a triumphant soldier. It might come to rest in the peaceful study of a philosopher bent over the composition of a book of wise sayings for the instruction of youth.

Before the seventh century B.C. the Jews do not seem to have had any written works which were recognized as official sacred books. They appealed to a living tradition which went back to Moses through the prophets, priests and kings. There were, of course, some writings which were carefully preserved, but they were not considered the final authority. However, by the end of that century the book of the *Law*, which consists of the first five books of our Bible, was accepted as containing the laws God has established for Israel.

Before the exile certain followers of the various prophets preserved copies of their sermons. These copies were carried into exile with the people and gave meaning and consolation to their lives in Babylon. Deprived of the Temple and its services the people delighted to gather in one another's homes and listen to the exiled priests reading from the words of the Prophets. Gradually, a whole collection of prophetical writings took form.

In the following centuries the books the Jews call the *Prophets*, (most of our prophetical books and some of our historical books) as well as the *Writings*, (all the other books) were gradually written and collected. By about 150 B.C. they too were considered as containing the writing of men inspired by the Spirit. About 90 A.D. the Jewish synod of Jamnia confirmed as sacred and unalterble the list of books which had been accepted for the past two centuries.

In the past there was a great deal of discussion about the differences between Catholic and Protestant Bibles. These differences came principally for three reasons. The first is that before 1943 the Vulgate (the Latin translation of the Bible made by St. Jerome in 384 A.D.) was the official Catholic Bible and all translations had to be made from it. Jerome had used the Septuagint or Greek version of the Old Testament which had more books in it than the Hebrew version. The Protestant Bible was translated from the original Hebrew. Thus the Catholic Bibles had 45 books in the Old Testament compared with 39 in the Protestant and Jewish Bibles.

But why does the Protestant Bible follow the Jewish listing? Probably the main reason is that at the time of the Reformation in the 16th century there was another movement abroad in Europe. It has been called the Renaissance. Briefly, it aroused a great interest in the past glories of the Greco-Roman civilization. Men began in great earnest to take up the study of the ancient languages of Greek and Hebrew. The Protestant Reformers, as we know, were very anxious to translate the Bible, known at the time mainly in the Latin translation of St. Jerome, into the various modern languages. The question arose as to which edition of the Bible to translate. Should they merely translate St. Jerome's Latin translation of the Bible into German or English? Should they translate the Septuagint which was a Greek version of the Old Testament? Or should they get back as close as possible to the original Bible as it came from the hands of the sacred authors? The answer was obvious; they would make a fresh translation from the Hebrew Bible itself. Unfortunately, it was not clearly realized that the Hebrew Bibles available to the reformers were copies which had been put together according to the decisions reached by the rabbis at Jamnia, who affirmed the Hebrew version.

The second reason is that translating is extremely difficult. Words often do not have the same meaning in two different languages. The translator has to have an accurate original source but he also has to make choices between the various shades of meaning of words and has to change the structure of the language to be faithful to the original meaning. In this process theological bias can play a part.

The third reason was that footnotes were added to the text to explain difficult passages. These reflected the theology of the translators and were often rather different.

Today Catholic, Protestant and Jewish translations are very, very close because scholars have more or less agreed on the best of the original sources and often work together in producing a translation. Very often Protestant and Jewish Bibles contain the extra six books of the Catholic Bible in a separate group entitled "Apocrypha" meaning books not having the same authority as the rest of the Bible.

There is no built-in norm for determining which books are inspired by God and which are not. The norm is ultimately some religious authority. The Hebrew text was accepted by those Jews who knew Hebrew, and the Greek text was accepted by the Jewish Community which spoke only Greek. The choice of the Greek text by the teaching authority of the Christian Church was expressed by the Council of Hippo in 393 A.D., and the Council of Carthage in 397 A.D. as well as in a letter by Pope Innocent I in 405 A.D. This choice was reaffirmed in a solemn pronouncement by the Council of Trent in 1546.

There are several popular Bibles on the market which attempt to put God's Word in simple modern language. These are not highly reliable translations and at times they do violence to the original.

LESSON 2

Semitic traders
(Egyptian tomb painting)

The Plan of God . . .
God Lays a Foundation

BEFORE YOU OPEN YOUR BIBLE

God is not remote, lost in the clouds of heaven. He shares our activity, our problems, our dreams. In the first lesson we saw that God has worked out a plan for our salvation. This plan is being carried out all around us in the world today.

But God had to make a start somewhere. He had to lay a foundation stone.

Our task: In this lesson we will find that God invites human beings with all their great qualities of soul, with their vision and vaulting ambitions, and with all their faults to work with him.

Where do we start? God made a beginning almost four thousand years ago with a nomad sheik named Abraham. We read his story in the Book of Genesis, chapters 12 to 25.

(For the moment we will leave aside the first eleven chapters of Genesis. They form a little book in themselves. A very important book, but one which has its own special problems. These problems make it difficult for the beginner to get the true meaning of the work, so we will discuss these chapters at a later time.)

NOW OPEN YOUR BIBLE AND READ:

BOOK OF GENESIS
Chapters 12 through 25

The story of Abraham: The whole of chapters 12 through 25 are very easy reading and well worth the time, but we are going to hit the high spots only. In these chapters God begins the working out of the great plan which is to reach fulfillment in Christ and the Church. It is the story of God's reaching out to humankind.

Although we realize that the stones which go to make up our parish church are as old as the world, the date we find on the cornerstone is the day on which construction was begun.

We know that there were countless generations of people before Abraham. But the Bible dates the history of God's people from the day when Abraham heard God's call and answered with trusting faith. On that day the cornerstone of the Church was laid.

behind the words

Background of these chapters: "Ur of the Chaldees", Abraham's original home, was a wealthy commercial center at the head of the Persian Gulf. It commanded the mouth of one of the great shipping channels which made Babylonia an important commercial power. Ur had a great temple dedicated to Nannar, the moon-god.

Abraham was a man of his times—a worshipper of the gods of the "Fertile Crescent". (Fertile Crescent is the name given to the lands which form the backdrop of nearly everything which happened in the Bible. If we draw a line from Egypt through Palestine and Syria and follow the Tigris from Euphrates valley to the Persian Gulf, we will have touched on practically all of the fertile land of the Middle East. The result is an unmistakable crescent-shaped line.)

In the time of Abraham the Fertile Crescent was host to a multitude of civilizations living side by side. This little sliver of green was the center of civilization from the Stone Age to the rise of Greece and Rome.

Such fertile land was also a tempting prize for the hardy barbarians of the mountains. As long as the governments of the crescent countries were strong the mountain peoples were kept out. But when civilization grew soft, as it had in Abraham's day (around 2000 B.C.), the invaders poured in and put everyone on the move.

After leaving Ur, Abraham became a "nomad". He and his tribe lived on the fringe of the desert. They hired out as migratory workers in time of peace and as paid soldiers in time of war.

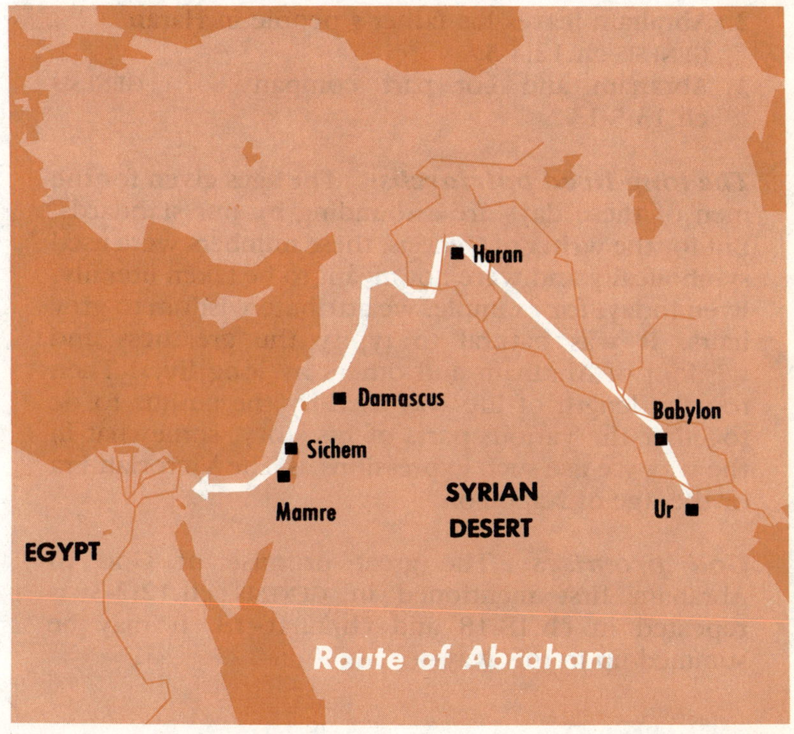

(These words sum up the contents of these chapters and also mark the great events in the life of Abraham.)

"Call" and "Promise"
— next to GENESIS ch.12
"Covenant"
— next to GENESIS ch.12
"Faith"
— next to GENESIS ch.22

understanding these selections

God calls: God's separation of his chosen one from the pagan surroundings of his first home takes place in three stages—

1. Abraham leaves Ur with his father and nephew . . . GENESIS ch.12:1-3
2. Abraham leaves his father's people in Haran . . . GENESIS ch.12:4-5
3. Abraham and Lot part company . . . GENESIS ch.13:5-13

The long-lived patriarchs: The ages given for the men of these days are astounding by our standards. But for the writer of Genesis, these numbers were used symbolically and were not meant to be taken literally. Even today, for example, we attribute wisdom to grey hairs. It was natural to typify the greatness and wisdom of Abraham and others by long lives. Then too the length of life was used by the author to tie together the various parts of his story, somewhat in the way we use such expressions as The Victorian Era or the Age of Napoleon.

God promises: The great promise of God to Abraham first mentioned in GENESIS ch.12:2-3 is repeated in ch.18:18 and ch.22:16-18. It may be summed up in this way—

1. He will have descendants more numerous than the stars.
2. They will possess a kingdom.
3. This kingdom will be the source of all good things for the whole of mankind.

Abraham's moral failure: The incident in Egypt, (GN. ch.12:12-20) serves as a good reminder that when God takes a human being as a partner he takes that person, faults and all, and gradually brings the chosen one to a state of full and perfect cooperation. In the meanwhile the person's faults may hinder the working out of God's plan, but only temporarily. Note that here as elsewhere the Bible never shies away from pointing out the faults even of God's most trusted servants.

Legal formalities of contracts in Abraham's day: (GN. ch.5:9-21) The ancient ceremony for making contracts was for the parties of the agreement to pass through the divided parts of an animal. The meaning behind the act was, "Let what has happened to this animal happen to the first one who breaks this agreement". Notice how God, having condescended to make a man his partner, adopts the ritual usual among the people of that time.

Abraham's driving away the birds of prey may have symbolized for the author the failure of human attempts to hinder the fulfillment of the divine promises.

The vision of Abraham: (GN. ch.15:17) The vision of the burning furnace stands for God.

Fire: God's spiritual nature, because it is the least material of the elements.

Smoke: The mystery of divinity, because of its impenetrability.

It should be remembered that the divine promises, as they affected Israel directly, were conditional upon fidelity to the Covenant.

The sacrifice of Isaac: (GN. ch.22:2)   In command-
ing such a sacrifice, God shows his supreme dominion
over all life.

In revoking the command, (GN. ch.22:12) God
shows that he does not wish people to express their
recognition of his dominion by human sacrifice. This
lesson was especially necessary for the people of Abraham's day as the practice of human sacrifice was quite
common then.

(GN. ch.22:15-18) The test was especially difficult,
as it was through Isaac that all God's promises were to
be carried out.

point of these selections from Genesis

We have grouped our readings for this lesson around
three key words: Call—Covenant—Faith. These three
words sum up the way in which God deals with us, the
way in which he works out his plan for our happiness
not only in history but right here and now.

Call: The whole of sacred history and of the life of
the individual with God depends entirely upon the in-
itiative of God.

Faith: But God has willed that his actions in history
have a consequence in our lives. God throws down
repeated challenges to which we must respond.

Covenant: The closeness and intimacy of God's activity with us is first expressed by the image of a con-
tract. Contracts are made between equals! Later God
will typify his dealings with us by the nuptial image,
the image of the bride and bridegroom.

the unity of the two testaments

(It has often been said that the best commentary on a
passage of the Bible is a passage from another part of
the Bible. Under this heading you will find the reflec-
tions of the New Testament writers upon the events

26

and persons of the Old Testament.)

In the New Testament we are shown how the great promises made to Abraham are fulfilled in Christ.

1. Abraham's *call* by God to be the father of a chosen race is confirmed, but now it is clear that it points to Christ and his work, (ST. JOHN'S GOSPEL, ch.8:51-59.)

2. Just as Abraham was able to enter into friendship with God through *faith*, so also we can enter into God's friendship only through the great gift of God, faith in his divine Son, (ST. PAUL'S LETTER TO THE ROMANS, ch.4:1-25.)

3. The *covenant* which rests on the "rock" Abraham (cf. ISAIAH ch.51:1-2) is replaced by a new covenant which rests on the "rock" Peter, (ST. MATTHEW'S GOSPEL, ch.16:18.)

4. The *promises* made to Abraham are actually worldwide in their fulfillment in Christ, (ST. PAUL'S LETTER TO THE GALATIANS, ch.3:7-29.)

5. The Church has always seen in the sacrifice of Isaac an image of the sacrifice of the Cross. (HEBREWS ch.11:17-19; ROMANS ch.8:32)

bible and church

The journey/pilgrimage of God's people begins as Abraham is promised the fulfillment of human desires: prosperity, land and fame. Over the centuries this hope for material values will gradually be transformed into promises of and hope for the spiritual values of love, peace, joy and everlasting life. Along the way God's people will, at times, make mistakes and fail miserably.

Today many people expect the Church not to make mistakes, but to be perfect and sinless. They expect that the Church would have learned from the mistakes of the past. Sometimes it does. Sometimes it does not. Abraham's moral failure in chapter 20 of Genesis shows that he had not learned much from his failure in chapter 12. And we see that Isaac does the same things in chapter 26 showing that he did not learn much from the mistakes of his forefathers.

Stories such as these are preserved in Scripture not as anti-hero statements, as found in so much of our modern literature and in many of our modern books of history and social commentary, but as a realistic recognition of the human condition. They are told with understanding and forgiveness and sometimes even with a touch of humor.

This same understanding and forgiveness is necessary when we see the faults, the failures and even the sins of individual Christians and especially of the leaders of the Church. Abraham is THE example of a man of faith. Yet at times he failed. The Church is a people of faith. They, too, fail at times. We may point out these failings and speak against them. But they should not be the occasion nor the reason for us to abandon the company of the church on the spiritual journey.

doers of the word

CALL: God continually calls individuals to become members of his chosen people. The Church has a prolonged program of initiation for these people. The Rite of Christian Initiation for Adults (R.C.I.A.) requires the help of active and dedicated Catholics. They are needed as sponsors, godparents, recruiters, hosts, and, at times, instructors. By offering your services to this program you will be helping others respond to the call of God.

FAITH: Making the Sign of the Cross and genuflecting is a deliberate and reverent way by which we proclaim our faith and by which we grow in faith.

COVENANT: The great Amen which is said at the end of the Consecration and just before the Our Father is our personal affirmation of the Covenant God has made with us through the blood of Jesus Christ. We should say it with vigor, with joy, with faith, realizing each time that we are renewing our commitment to the New Covenant.

1. How and when did God begin to work out his plan for our happiness?

____

____

2. What are three key words which sum up God's method of working out his plan?

a.____________Where is this described in Genesis?

____

b.____________Where is this described in Genesis?

____

c.____________Where is this described in Genesis?

____

3. What was the double lesson God wanted to teach by the command to sacrifice Isaac?

a. ___________________________________

____

b. ___________________________________

____

4. How are the promises made to Abraham fulfilled in Christ?

____

____

1. In what sense are we children of Abraham?

2. If we are children of Abraham, what is our relationship to the Jews?

3. How would you describe what faith means in your life?

4. What experiences have you had when it seemed that God was calling you to do something foolish or destructive to your hopes as he did when he commanded Abraham to sacrifice Isaac? How did they turn out?

MOVING ON

. . . Abraham to Jacob

The story of God's people is the story of how individuals respond to God's choice of them. Abraham responds with faith when he is called by God. He leaves some of his family behind in Ur, others in Haran. Later he even parts from his nephew Lot (GN. 13). However, Abraham's allegiance to his family roots remains strong (GN. 14). When the time comes for Isaac to marry, a wife is sought for him among the family in Haran (GN. 24).

The continuation of God's promise and blessings is a free gift that does not depend on human decisions and human values. When Sara does not give Abraham an heir, he decides to turn to her maidservant to have a descendent promised by God (GN. 16). This failure to rely on God leads to discontent and division in the family. When Yahweh blesses Sara with a child, the older son Ismael is passed over in favor of Isaac, the son of the free-woman, but God still blesses Ismael (GN. 21).

The story of the next generation shows that human values count for nothing; God's decision is all important. Esau, the elder and favorite of his father Isaac, shows little respect for his birthright and sells it to his younger brother, Jacob, who lacks the macho qualities his father admires (GN. 25). Once Isaac recognizes and accepts what has happened, he makes arrangements to find a wife for Jacob among the family in Haran.

God brings good out of seemingly impossible situations in the lives of those he has chosen. After dealing patiently and cleverly with his uncle Laban, Jacob comes back with two wives and twelve sons (GN. 29-31). Leah, the less favored, bears him ten sons: Rachel, his beloved, bears two sons upon whom his father unwisely dotes. This, not surprisingly, leads to dissension; Joseph, spoiled and imprudent in dealing with his older brothers, becomes a victim of their jealousy (GN. 37).

They sell him into slavery and he is carried off to Egypt. There he grows both through his willfulness and his fidelity to become a powerful man in the land (GN. 34-41). His power becomes a means of saving his famine-afflicted family for the destiny God has in mind for them. Joseph brings his brothers to a land of exile where they prosper for a time in preparation for the journey/pilgrimage back through the desert with Moses.

Rameses II

The Birth of the Nation

BEFORE YOU OPEN YOUR BIBLE

God had now laid the foundation of his plan for his people's happiness. With perfect freedom he chose one man and made a promise to him. In this lesson you will learn how God began to make good on this promise.

The fulfillment of God's plan, as you know, is Christ in his Church. All that Moses had done for the enslaved Hebrews, Jesus was to do for all people enslaved to sin.

Our task: Now our task is to become familiar with the great saving act of God in the pages of the Book of Exodus. This will deepen our understanding of the great saving acts of Christ and his Church in the pages of the New Testament and in our daily life.

NOW OPEN YOUR BIBLE AND READ:

BOOK OF EXODUS
Chapter 2:1 through Chapter 14:22

behind the words

What went before: Around 1850 B.C., Abraham had heard the call of Yahweh, as the Hebrews called God, and received the promise. Isaac, the child of promise, passed the torch of faith to his son Jacob who settled in the Land of Goshen (in the northeastern part of Egypt) around 1700 B.C. This fertile country was ideal for sheep raising, and the seventy members of the tribe and their servants settled down under the protection of the Hyksos dynasty. Before "returning to his fathers" Jacob blessed his son, Juda, and announced that the Messiah would be born of his line.

Reason for the sojourn in Egypt: In this secluded corner of Egypt there was less danger of the little tribe's losing its new-found monotheistic faith. Their contact with the ancient civilization of Egypt would do much to bring out in the little clan of Abraham those elements from which a nation, the People of God, could be formed.

What happens here: With the appearance of Moses the record of God's dealings with his people takes a decisive step. God will turn the unorganized horde of refugees into his people.

The Hyksos Pharaohs: This Egyptian dynasty was not Egyptian at all! The Hyksos Pharaohs were semitic in origin, like Abraham and his family, and had conquered Egypt during a period of Egypt's internal decay. When the Egyptians finally threw off the foreign yoke under the Rameses, they weren't slow in punishing any former friends of their hated masters. This bit of history explains why the Jews first found a haven and then slavery in the land of Egypt.

WRITE IN THE MARGIN OF YOUR BIBLE THE FOLLOWING KEY WORDS:

"Call of Moses"
— next to EXODUS ch.3:2
"Passover"
— next to EXODUS ch.12:1

understanding these selections

THE CALL (EXODUS ch.3:2-4:23)

The mountain of the Lord: (EX. ch.3:1)   It is interesting to note that the scene of the Call, Horeb or Sinai, is the same as that of the giving of the Law. That God is represented in the vision by fire is fitting because among the ancients, fire was thought to be the least material of the elements.

Holy ground: (EX. ch.3:5)   The practice of removing the shoes is a common Middle Eastern sign of reverence. The Moslems still observe this practice whenever entering a Mosque.

Holy name: (EX. ch.3:14)   The divine name, Yahweh, expresses the perfect and complete independence of God. The ancient Hebrews, not being philosophers, did not, in all probability, see the metaphysical implications in the divine name. That God is by nature essentially existing and hence in no way dependent upon anyone else would be too abstract an idea for them. The Hebrews probably understood God's independence concretely in reference to his independent activity on behalf of his chosen people.

Making bricks in Egypt
(tomb painting)

Pharaoh's free will: (EX. ch.4:21) The continual references to God's hardening Pharaoh's heart is due to the sacred writers' practice of looking to the primary cause of things, God, with a certain loss of emphasis on the secondary causes, in this case Pharaoh's greed and pride.

The Hebrew expression might better be rendered "Pharaoh became stubborn." When an apple fell from a tree in the orchard because of the law of gravity, the Hebrew would say that God had plucked the apple from the tree. This makes pretty good sense, in a way, for the law of gravity is after all only an expression of the divine Will.

THE PASSOVER (EXODUS ch.12:1-13:22)

The passover meal: (EX. ch.12:1-20) The details of the preparation of the lamb are significant. "Roasting" is the quickest way of preparing the lamb. The "bitter herbs", probably wild endive and wild lettuce, point up the bitterness of oppression. The way in which the meal was to be eaten, standing with staff in hand, also indicated the hastiness and readiness for departure. The bread is unleavened for there isn't time to wait for the dough to rise.

How many people left? (EX. ch.12:37) The number of Israelites departing from Egypt seems too large to have crossed by a ford in a single night and is almost equivalent to the population of the whole of Palestine in the year 1922. In another place we are told that the number of Israelites was too small to settle the whole of Palestine at one time. For these reasons it seems that the number given has been miscopied in the course of time.

A perpetual reminder: (EX. ch.12:43-13:15) The "law of azymes and firstborn" was intended to be a perpetual reminder to the people of the great saving act which God had done for them on the eve of their escape from bondage.

The presentation of Jesus in the Temple was done

36

in obedience to this law of the firstborn. And St. Paul speaks about the law of the azymes in I CORINTHIANS ch.5:7-8 where he refers to Easter as the new Passover.

A pious custom: (EX. ch.13:16)   Here is the origin of the custom of wearing "phylacteries," small leather boxes containing little scrolls upon which was written certain scriptural passages. These little boxes were bound to the forehead and arm during prayer by leather thongs, (cf. also DEUTERONOMY ch.6 and ch.11). Our Lord upbraided the Pharisees for their ostentation and hypocrisy in observing this custom. (MATTHEW ch.23:5.)

The route of the exodus: The Israelites were directed to take the longer route around the Sinai peninsula because this less traveled route would avoid the customs stations and garrisons of soldiers which abounded along the great coastal highway between Egypt and Canaan.

THE CROSSING (EXODUS ch.14:1-22)

The great miracle of the exodus: The exact method by which the Israelites crossed the Sea is uncertain, but the combination of circumstances which enabled them to make their escape was certainly providential to the point of being miraculous.

In other words, the real miracle is not so much the precise way in which they crossed as in the fact that God provided this means of escape just at the moment when it was needed.

The crossing of the Red Sea by the Israelites was to make a great impression on future generations of Jews as is shown from the constant reference to it throughout the rest of Sacred Scripture. It became for the Jews the great symbol of God's special care for his people.

It is interesting to note that the Jews probably crossed the "Reed" Sea and that our present reading of "Red" Sea is due to a mistake made in copying the text. The Reed Sea was probably a group of smaller bodies of water to the North of the Red Sea. It was a low treacherous area dotted with lakes, lagoons, canals and papyrus swamps.

point of these selections from Exodus

We might summarize these selections by saying that they stress the social nature of the People of God, in the Old Testament, foreshadowing the unity of the Mystical Body of Christ, the Church. That is, the individual Jews were freed from the bondage of Egypt precisely because they belonged to the people of God.

The other great lesson is the awesome power of God's will that "all men be saved and brought to the knowledge of salvation." In the great miracles of the Exodus, the plagues, the crossing, the manna and water in the desert, we see how wholeheartedly God had committed himself to his plan of bringing people back to his friendship.

the unity of the two testaments

The new Moses: It was the vocation of Moses to be the mediator or go-between of God and his people. Christ perfects this vocation and is the "New Moses," (GOSPEL OF ST. JOHN ch.1:17, and EPISTLE TO THE HEBREWS ch.3:1-19).

The Law of Moses: God's law, given through Moses, remains valid but possesses a *new meaning* for the Christian. Christ, on the Mount of the Beatitudes, like Moses on Mt. Sinai, gives to the Christian the Law of God. (GOSPEL OF ST. MATTHEW ch.5:1-48)

bible and church

The Church, which is the Mystical Body of Christ, rescues people from the slavery of sin by helping them be open to the call of faith and by leading them through the waters of Baptism to the freedom of a new life in Christ. To do this task the Church does more than preach about Jesus. It also tries to liberate people from poverty and all forms of oppression which make it so difficult for people to hear the Word

38

of God.

Moses found it necessary to give his people a Law so that they could live up to their calling as God's people. So too today, the Church continually tries to show people how to live the Commandments God gave Moses on Mt. Sinai and the Christian Law given by Jesus in the Sermon on the Mount.

There is some opposition to and controversy about the way the Pope and the bishops interpret and apply these laws. However, in raising and speaking on moral issues they are trying to help people lead lives which will truly free them from the slavery of sin and bring them into the promised land, of eternal life.

doers of the word

God brought his people to freedom through the instrumentality of a human being, Moses. Today he is still trying to free his people through the instrumentality of other people, namely us.

We can help people find the freedom of the children of God by sharing our faith stories with them and by actively participating in Evangelization and R.C.I.A. programs.

We can lead people from the slavery of ignorance to the knowledge of the one true God and his Son, Jesus Christ, by learning more about the Scriptures and about our faith and by sharing what we learn with others.

We can help lead people from the slavery of poverty by helping those in need of food, clothing, and shelter, and by working with others who are seeking to promote economic justice.

We can help free people from the tyranny of the fear of a nuclear holocaust by working for disarmament and world peace.

Often too, we can help people who are addicted to alcohol or drugs by leading them to programs such as A.A.

With a little reflection each of us can think of little ways in which we can help people find freedom and a promised land so they may be able to serve God better.

questions

1. What new development does God's plan for our salvation undergo in the Book of Exodus?

____

2. What three words best sum up the big events of the Book of Exodus?

a_______________ b_______________ c_______________

3. What does "Yahweh" mean?

____

____

4. Why were the Hyksos kings important in the history of God's People?

____

____

5. What was *the* saving act of Yahweh for the Jews?

____

topics for discussion

1. Discuss the character of Moses. What kind of man was he? Illustrate by examples from the Bible text. To whom would you compare him today?

2. Why do you think an appreciation of the Exodus is important for the Christian as well as for the Jew?

3. Why do you or do you not think that the events related in the story of the Exodus occurred in exactly the way they were recorded?

4. What have been "Exodus" experiences in your live when you have passed from sort of "slavery" to a new life?

MOVING ON

When we look at God's ways of preparing leaders for his people they often seem strange until we see them in the light of subsequent events. Moses is prepared for his role in freeing the people in a most unlikely way. He is raised in the court of Pharaoh but has to flee into the desert where he becomes a shepherd and gets to know the territory (EX. 2).

When God's call comes, Moses, like many other prophets and leaders, is reluctant to accept the responsibility, but the narrative tells us, with some humor, how God patiently overcomes his excuses. Moses feels he cannot speak well so God tells him to have his brother Aaron be the spokesman. But by the time of the fourth plague we see Moses becoming confident and speaking for himself (EX. 7-8).

A close reading of the story of the plagues reveals a careful structure. Plagues similar to those mentioned in the text were frequent natural occurrences in Egypt. The writer telescopes a series of these events to show that through nature God reveals his greatness to those who believe. The story begins with *water*, the source of life, from which frogs and mosquitoes emerge. The *air* is filled with gadflies and with germs which cause boils; hail falls from the *heavens* and locusts fill the *earth*. The whole earth, plants, animals, and humanity are afflicted and finally plunged into the darkness of a sandstorm and into the ultimate tragedy of death (EX. 7-11).

As the story unfolds, Pharaoh's magicians are wise enough to see that they are only doubling the damage and bringing more suffering on themselves. They pull out of the contest. Pharaoh remains blinded by his pride, even after his courtiers and the people come to their senses and advise him to recognize the power of Yahweh.

LESSON 4

Legal code of Hammurabi

"Thy Law Is My Delight"

BEFORE YOU OPEN YOUR BIBLE

The vocation of Moses was the vocation of Israel in miniature. That the place where Moses first heard the call of God and the place where Israel was to seal its covenant with God were one and the same (Mt. Sinai) was no accident. It was Moses' mission to lead one people out of the misery of slavery. It was the mission of that people to be the channel of salvation for all people.

Our task: We need to understand the nature of Israel's mission as expressed in the covenant of Sinai, and to see how the covenant was worked out through the Law. Another way of putting it might be that we need to discover the place of the Law in the life of the people and of the individual.

OPEN YOUR BIBLE AND READ:

> BOOK OF DEUTERONOMY,
> Chapter 4:1-40 and Chapters 26:1 through
> Chapter 30:20

(You may also wish to read the account of the giving of the Law as found in the Book of Exodus, ch. 19-24.)

behind the words

For the first time in our reading of the Bible we come across one of its great themes, "THE LAW". This expression embodied for the pious Israelite a way of life which if observed carefully assured one of God's favor. Since this idea of the Law, as embodying a whole way of life, is so basic to an understanding of the Old Testament it is worthwhile to examine briefly the Law of Moses.

In origin it drew upon the common law of the whole Middle East, but it has an elevated tone and spiritual quality which sets it far above other legal codes of its day. Its idea of justice, while often harsh to the modern reader, was quite merciful by the standards of the day. One of the most outstanding qualities of the Hebrew Law Code was its concern for the weak and defenseless, the widow and the orphan, and its insistence on the dignity of woman.

Its most unique quality is that it pictures God as above and beyond his creation. It totally rejected the view of other religions of the day. They confused or identified God with the forces of nature.

Our legal expressions are often highly technical. The laws of the State of Illinois, for example, make dry reading for the layman. The Jews, however, often placed their laws in a historical framework. Sometimes a historical event will offer motives for obeying

Mount Sinai

the law, or a practical application of the law, in order to make the particular law more meaningful to the people who are expected to observe it.

The message of Deuteronomy: This book, which is cast in the form of a series of addresses or sermons of Moses to the people on the threshold of their entry into the promised land, contains some of the most sublime words on true morality. Its message might be summed up in this way— love and righteousness go together. To love God means also to love and deal justly and uprightly with one's neighbor.

It tells of the one true God who is a *living* God not wrought of wood or stone. He is a *jealous* God in that he cannot remain indifferent when his people turn away from him. He is a *loving* God in that he has exercised the most amazing providence in behalf of his chosen people. And he has chosen them not because they were the most numerous of the people of the earth, and not because they had always been his faithful servants, for just the opposite was often the case. But because he had loved them and was determined to keep his promises to their fathers.

The people in their turn must *fear,* that is reverence, him as the great and mighty God upright and just in all his ways. But most of all they must re-

turn *love* for love. They must give an intense, personal devotion which seeks to give undivided loyalty in every phase of life.

WRITE IN THE MARGIN OF YOUR BIBLE THE FOLLOWING KEY WORDS:

    ''Keep God's Law?''—Moses preaches a sermon
— next to DEUTERONOMY ch.4:1
''The Widow and the Orphan''—the wedding of worship and social justice
— next to DEUTERONOMY ch.26:1
''Choose Life''—Moses last appeal
— next to DEUTERONOMY ch.30:1

understanding these selections

Inspired commentary: (DT. ch.4:1-40)   Deuteronomy forms what might be called an ''inspired commentary'' on the events of the Exodus. It shows the meaning behind the events. It has been called the purest form of historical writing as the Jews understood this type of writing. For the Jew historical writing was not a mere reporting of events and dates but rather an explanation of the significance of the events. We would call this a philosophy or theology of history.

    The passage chosen here is one of the most beautiful in the book. It is a beautiful and eloquent expression of wonder at God's loving care for his people.

The cloud: (DT. ch.4:11-12) The cloud which covered the mountain top and the thunder and lightning were a visible sign of God's presence.

Prohibition against idolotry: (DT. ch.4:15) The repeated prohibition against representing God in some material form was to emphasize God's spiritual nature. Because of the people's idolatrous background and the pagan world they lived in there was great danger of backsliding into idolatry.

the unity of the two testaments

The influence of the Book of Deuteronomy was very great, so it is not surprising that it is quoted some thirty-two times in the New Testament. If we add the number of times it is alluded to or quoted indirectly we find some one hundred and twelve passages in the New Testament.

When Jesus was asked which was the most important of the commandments (MARK ch.12:29-30) he immediately answered by quoting Deuteronomy ch.6:4-6.

During the forty days in the desert when the devil appeared to Christ to tempt him we also find our Lord turning to the words of Deuteronomy to answer Satan. (MATTHEW ch.4:4,7,10—LUKE ch.4:4,8,12).

Jesus also recalls his hearers to the true spirit of Deuteronomy when he warns them of the danger of an exclusively legalistic approach to God. Such an approach, while outwardly free from blame, actually dispenses with the very heart of a truly moral life, repentance and the total gift of self to God. (MATTHEW ch.23:1-39). On this same subject St. Paul tells his followers that it is faith which supports the law and brings it to perfection. (ROMANS ch.3:7-31 and GALATIANS ch.5:13—ch.6:18).

bible and church

The Law of Moses was based on the best of the laws of the peoples with which the Hebrews had contact. Moses' unique contribution to law was giving an entirely different reason for observing it. Other peoples observed their laws because the king had made them. Moses made the observance of the law a religious act. It was a way to know, love and serve the one, true God and to become united as his people.

The motive behind the observance of the Law of God was always love because God is a God of love. At times people saw him as a God of fear, and then they observed the Law because of his justice and fear of punishment rather than as a sign of their love for him.

Jesus showed the people that justice, mercy, obedience, and reverential fear are one with love and are not incompatible as we sometimes think them to be.

Church laws are intended to help people know, love and serve God and to stay united as his people. They have arisen from centuries of experience. For example, the law on Sunday Mass arose from a realization that a person who, without a good reason, does not join the community at least weekly is not manifesting very much faith in Jesus and love for what he has done for us.

However, we can fall into the same temptation of legalism as some of the Jews did. We can think that the external observance of the letter of the law makes us pleasing to God, forgetting that the essential ingredient is a spirit of returning love for love.

If we feel that the Commandments, the Beatitudes and Church laws are a hindrance and burden, we may well question the degree of our love for God.

doers of the word

The regular and frequent celebration of the Sacrament of Reconciliation is intended to have us reflect on how well we have observed the Law of God, to love him above all else and to love our neighbor as ourselves.

It is a time to ask ourselves how we have failed to keep the Law and ask forgiveness from God and from the community.

It is a time to ask ourselves whether we keep the Law merely from habit or as an expression of our love for God.

It is a time to ask ourselves deeper questions about the fears, the pride, the anger, etc. which make it so difficult to keep the Law.

Finally, it is a time to recall God's love, mercy and forgiveness which have never failed and which will never fail.

questions

1. What fact gives us a hint of the similarity between the mission of Moses and that of the people as a

whole?

2. What was the unique contribution of the Mosaic Law?

3. What was the meaning of "THE LAW" to the ancient Jews?

4. What was the main purpose of the Book of Deuteronomy?

5. How does the concept of God in Deuteronomy differ from that of the pagan world?

topics for discussion

1. Read DEUTERONOMY ch.26:16-19. What do these verses suggest to you about the nature of God and the motives people should have for observing the Law?

2. Why do you think Jesus could say that the entire Law of Moses is summed up in the one command, to love God and neighbor?

3. Which law do you think is easier to keep, the detailed Law laid out in Deuteronomy or the overall law of love?

4. Why isn't the law of love a license to do what we please as long as we feel that we are doing it out of love?

LESSON 5

Canaanite god

"A Land Flowing with Milk and Honey"

God is faithful! Those words ring out down through the course of the Old Testament. In the two books we are now going to read, Joshua and Judges, we will see how God acts with perfect fidelity in carrying out his promises. This is the main theme of the Book of Joshua. At the same time we are struck by the fact that the promised land was not handed to the people of God on a silver platter. The conquest of Canaan, the land flowing with milk and honey, was a long and bitter struggle. The people suffered defeat and virtual enslavement on many occasions.

This side of their history was not overlooked by the Jews either. The Book of Judges was written to answer an objection. If God was as faithful to his promises as the sacred authors claimed, why was the possession of the Promised Land gained at such a terrible cost and so transitory and uncertain a possession at best?

God's workshop: Another question which naturally occurs to us is "Why was it so important for the People of God to possess a land in the first place?" The key to this puzzle lies in God's over-all purpose, the creation of his Church. To carry forward the work of creating a channel of salvation through a gradual education of his people to their task, an atmosphere of stability and continuity was essential. In short, God needed a workshop in which to hammer out and perfect his vessel of election. The land of Canaan was to be that workshop.

Our task: The whole history of God's dealings with people points up clearly that God has paid them the magnificent compliment of making them partners in the work of salvation. Briefly, God needs people. This truth is strikingly illustrated in the two books under consideration. Here you will see in the concrete just how this partnership works, and the demands it makes on both partners.

The riches of the Bible: There are several other very interesting themes running through these two books. One is the strong emphasis on the community and solidarity of the people of God. This is, in a primitive and almost barbaric form, the first outlines of the People of God, united in Christ. Here too we find examples of that universality of salvation and the responsibility of the individual under God which will reach their full flowering in the New Testament.

As you read through the assigned chapters see if you can pick out examples of these themes:

1. *The moral unity or solidarity of the community,* that is, all the members of the nation share in the rewards or punishments of the nation's fidelity or infidelity to the covenant with Yahweh.

2. ***The will of God that everyone be saved*** and that Israel is not the only beneficiary of the divine plan.

3. ***The personal moral responsibility*** of the individual, that is, each member of the Hebrew nation will also be judged on his or her own fidelity to the Covenant.

NOW OPEN YOUR BIBLE AND READ:
BOOK OF JOSHUA
Chapters 1 through 7, and Chapters 23-24
BOOK OF JUDGES,
Chapter 2, and Chapters 13 through 16

behind the words

Joshua and Judges compared. The first of these two books might be called "Epic History." It paints with a broad brush and hits only the highlights of a military campaign in Canaan. The emphasis is placed on the essential event: God has promised his people a land of their own and now he fulfills his promise.

The Book of Judges, on the other hand, is more down to earth. It concentrates on the steps which lay between promise and fulfillment—the slow, painful infiltration, the habitual infidelity to the Covenant which brought in its wake defeat and subjection.

The two books cover roughly the same period and the same events but from two different points of view. Joshua lays the emphasis on the acts of God, while Judges examines the acts of men and women. The two accounts are complementary, not contradictory. Together they fill in for us the fascinating story of the invasion of Canaan.

Canaan at the time of the invasion, c. 1000 B.C. The Canaanites were a wealthy and highly civilized people. They lived in strongly fortified towns from which they would go out to work their farms. Politically the country was swarming with tiny city-states all of which owed a loose sort of allegiance to Egypt.

At the time of the invasion the country was suffering from internal decay. There were but two classes, the very rich and the very poor. Religion was a sorry thing. The Canaanite gods were worshipped largely for what the worshipper could get out of it. Sacrifices were looked upon as so many bribes to the god in order to get rain or a good harvest, etc. In short it might be called a religion of "self-interest" in which immorality and human sacrifice had a part. The victims were usually infants, the aged, or prisoners of war who were burned or buried alive.

The investigation of the archeologists have shed a good deal of light on this period and offer many interesting confirmations of the authenticity of the accounts in Joshua and Judges. By their diligent exploration archeologists have pretty well established, for instance, that the site of Jericho is by far the oldest center of urban life in the world. Its remains go back more than nine thousand years to when people first began building fortified permanent dwellings.

Archeologists have uncovered the remains of city walls destroyed by fire or earthquake. At first they speculated that these were the walls which fell when the horns blew in the last part of the twelfth century B.C. Now they have established that those walls fell over a hundred years before Joshua arrived in Canaan. The biblical account is more religious than historical. It tells us that God gave the land to the Hebrews and helped them conquer it.

WRITE IN THE MARGIN OF YOUR BIBLE THE FOLLOWING KEY PASSAGES:

"The Battle of Jericho"
— next to JOSHUA ch.1
"Joshua's Last Words"
— next to JOSHUA ch.23
"A Warning Unheeded"
— next to JUDGES ch.2
"A Popular Hero"
— next to JUDGES ch.13

The Battle of Jericho: (JOS. ch.1-6)   The crossing of the Jordon (JOS. ch.3:14-4:18) recalls the crossing of the Red Sea under Moses and serves much the same purpose, namely to confirm Joshua as the divinely appointed leader of the people. It would seem that the miracle of the blockage of the upper waters was a providential act of God rather than a strict miracle. We have at least two other examples of this drying up of the Jordan which were perfectly natural in origin from relatively modern history, in 1267 A.D. and again in 1927. The phenomenon seems due to the undermining of the banks by the waters of the river so that from time to time a large section collapses into the stream and dams off the waters. That it happened at the particular moment when the Jews were preparing to invade Canaan and the people had foreknowledge of the event clearly shows the finger of God and is the real miracle in the event.

The whole description of the Battle of Jericho, (JOS. ch.6:2-26), has something of the flavor of a religious service, with the priests marching at the head of the army carrying the Ark of the Covenant and the sound of trumpets. Do we perhaps find a reminder in these trumpet tones of the sound of the trumpet mentioned in the New Testament which will herald the last day when judgment will be passed forever upon the wicked?

It may well be that the New Testament writers had in mind the ancient practice of proclaiming a ''ban'' or ''herem'' against one's enemies in wars which is probably what was taking place at Jericho when the people shouted and the trumpets sounded.

The institution of the ''ban'' (JOS. 6:21,26) was always linked with religious wars among the ancients of the Near East. The enemy, his cities, his possessions, families, and slaves were ''dedicated,'' i.e. destroyed or slain, to the god. A similar custom existed among some of our own ancestors, for in the period of the late Roman empire certain Germanic tribes acted in the same way. The "ban" was a law of warfare in an iron age which had never heard of international law or the Geneva Convention for the humane treatment of prisoners of war.

The emphasis placed on this custom in the time of Joshua was due to the extreme danger of religious and moral contamination. That this danger was real is clear from the first chapters of Judges.

The cruelty of this ancient institution, a common heritage of the near Eastern peoples, was gradually ameliorated among the people of God as God led them along the road of moral education.

Joshua's last words: (JOS. ch.23-24)   Here we have a summary of the theme of the whole book. The ageing general sums up his life's work and warns the people of the danger of contamination by contact with the idolatrous and licentious practices of their Canaanite neighbors. He recalls for the people all of the love and care which God has lavished upon them since the time of Abraham and calls for their unswerving loyalty to Yahweh and his covenant.

A warning unheeded: (JGS. ch. 2)   In this chapter we have an introduction to the whole book which points up the religious interpretation of Jewish history. Behind the individual events a definite pattern is seen: Sin—Punishment—Repentance—Deliverance.

The leaders of the people were called "judges" as this was one of their chief duties, deciding disputes, but by no means their only one. The Hebrew word for judges might better be translated as "champions". The Judges were true national heroes.

A popular hero: (JGS. ch.13-16)   Here we have a perfect example of the popular hero. He is brave, has a fatal weakness for the fairer sex, and is gifted with an earthy wit and sense of humor. He also illustrates in his own life the four steps of the pattern of sin, punishment, repentance, and deliverance mentioned above.

the unity of the two testaments

The cry "hosanna!" is familiar to Christians. We hear it in the "glad tidings" of the angels at the birth of Christ and in the cry of the children on the first Palm Sunday.

But few realize that it comes from the Hebrew verb "to save" and means "Save Now!"

Christ is preeminently "He who saves". And it was no accident that he was given the name "Jesus" or "Joshua", meaning "God's Salvation". For just as Joshua led one people into a land of their own, so Jesus leads us into heaven.

The Jews of our Lord's day revered Joshua as one of their great national saviors, for it was he who had led the people into the land of promise.

In the Letter to the Hebrews, the sacred writer reminds his readers of God's promise to their ancestors. The promise of a land of their own. He explains that this promise has now been more wondrously fulfilled in the Christian's hope of heaven that it ever was in the days of Joshua (HEBREWS ch.11:8-16).

bible and church

Jesus has led us into the Promised Land of the kingdom of God. The Church is the most complete, visible sign of that kingdom on earth. We can view it ideally and see it as the work of God's grace, the sign of God's presence, the instrument of the Spirit, a material and spiritual success. But at the same time, as in the story of the Judges, the reality must also be acknowledged; grace is ignored, selfishness promotes negative reactions, pride divides the members and isolates them one from the other. The ideal is seldom realized. The Christian community soars to great heights and slides to abysmal lows at one and the same time.

But the Church continues in its strengths and its weaknesses. It provides for continual but gradual growth because its foundation stone, Jesus, is always present. In its weaknesses we learn of our need for God. In its strengths we realize that his power is working through us.

Within our limitations of time, space and understanding God continues to work through us to transform and change the world. The history of the Church, like the history of the Israelites, is at once an epic of grandeur and heroism and at the same time one of human tragedy and comedy.

doers of the word

In these readings we have seen the crucial position of the divinely appointed leaders of the People of God, their difficult tasks, their human failings.

We, who belong to the New People of God, also have divinely appointed leaders in the Pope and bishops of the Church, successors of the Twelve. Let us pray for them daily for the tasks set them today are no less awe-inspiring than those which faced Joshua and the Judges in Israel.

A simple prayer which we can say for the Pope is that which is found in the Liturgy of Good Friday:

"Almighty and eternal God, you guide all things by your word, you govern all Christian people. In your love protect the Pope you have chosen for us. Under his leadership deepen our faith and make us better Christians. We ask this through Christ our Lord."

For the bishop we might say: "Lord our God, you have chosen your servant our bishop to be a shepherd of your flock in the tradition of the apostles. Give him a spirit of courage and right judgment, a spirit of knowledge and love. By governing with fidelity those entrusted to his care may he build your Church as a sign of salvation for the world. Grant this through our Lord Jesus Christ, your Son, who lives and reigns with you and the Holy Spirit, one God, for ever and ever."

questions

1. What is the main theme of the Book of Joshua?

2. Why is the Book of Judges so called?

____

3. In what way does it differ from the Book of Joshua in its approach to the record of the events of the Conquest of Canaan?

____

4. Why was it so important in the working out of God's plan for the People to possess a land?

____

5. What three ideas which were to be so important in the message of the Gospels do we already see hinted at in these Books?

a. ____

b. ____

c. ____

topics for discussion

1. What is your reaction to the "herem" in Hebrew warfare? (ch.6:18 and 21; ch.7:1-26.) Do you see any modern parallels?

2. What do you think of the following statement?—"The entire history of the conquest of the Promised Land is a prophecy of the spiritual conquest of the world through the Church under the leadership of Jesus the Messiah."

3. Can you think of a example from your life or the life of someone you know which seems to illustrate the pattern of Sin-Punishment-Repentence-Deliverance?

4. What value do you see for your own life from reading the Book of Joshua and of Judges?

5. Which of the stories about the Judges is your favorite? Why?

BACKGROUND:

The Land of the Bible

God chose very small quarters to set up his workshop; The Holy Land is roughly the size of the state of Vermont. It is about 150 miles long and from 28 miles wide in the North to 54 miles in the South.

The country falls into three natural divisions. Along the coast is the *Maritime Plain*. This is a narrow ribbon along the coast. It boasts no real harbors, which helps to explain why the Jews never became sailors.

Bordering this coastal plain is the hill country. While the hills are too low to be called mountains, they are craggy and rugged. They form a very effective barrier against invading armies. And since the Plain of Esdraelon lying to the south of Galilee is the only means of easy access to the interior of the country from West to East and thus provides a passage from Egypt to Babylon, it is a natural battlefield and its fertile ground has been watered with the blood of countless generations of soldiers.

Beyond the hill-country the land is slashed by the dizzying gorge of the Jordan River which flows from the foothills of Mt. Hermon, a real snow-clad mountain, to the torrid desert surrounding the Dead Sea.

The climate ranges from sub-tropical to desert. And while the average temperature ranges from 68 to 73, temperatures as high as 130 have been noted in the Jordan Gorge. In the inland areas it has ranged from below freezing to 80 in a single day!

This area was certainly well suited to the plan of God for it was really at the center of things. It was the crossroads of the two great empires of the ancient world, Babylonian and Egyptian. Yet, at the same time, it was relatively isolated by its semi-mountainous terrain.

MOVING ON:

The Book of Judges presents us with a mixed bag of heroes, very human at times in their pride and selfishness. Yet they were called by Yahweh to be his instruments for the salvation of his people. Men like Barak are weak and timid. Women like Deborah and Jael are confident and courageous (JGS. 4). Gideon knows little about Yahweh and plays childish games with God (JGS. 6). When he is victorious he takes the credit himself and leads his people into idolotry (JGS. 7-8). Jephthah is certainly very pagan in his understanding of Yahweh (JGS. 11), and Samson hardly knows him at all. This most famous of the Judges is physically strong but spiritually weak. Spoiled and willful, Samson begins in a blindness of spirit that eventually leads to physical blindness; only then can he begin to see as a man of faith.

The last words of this book describe the sad plight of Israel estranged from its God, "and every man did as he pleased." This is the condition described in the opening of the books of Samuel. There is darkness over the land and the light of Yahweh flickers but dimly in people like Elkana, Hanna and Eli.

Then came Samuel, the last of the judges and the first of the prophets. He is ready to listen and to speak out for the Lord. Slowly he brings about a revival of the spiritual life of the Israelites who turn away from their pagan gods and once more follow Yahweh. As usual, the fervor declines as Samuel grows old. His sons do not follow his ways, and the people ask for a king (I SM. 8). The first king is tall and handsome, physically impressive to the people. Saul, like Samson, is willful and knows little about Yahweh. Even though the Spirit works through him, he himself cannot tune into the mind and heart of the Lord. Pride and selfishness again predominate. As a result of Saul's hardness of heart, David, a man after God's heart, is chosen to replace him.

LESSON 6

Son of David

"A family record of Jesus Christ, son of David, son of Abraham."

MATTHEW ch.1:1

BEFORE YOU OPEN YOUR BIBLE

God works out his plan: God started the job of restoring the human race to friendship by choosing one man, Abraham, whose family was to be the keepers of the flame of faith down through the ages. Gradually under the influence of God's activity the little band of wanderers became a united people bound to God by vows of fidelity. But to preserve this group as the people of God they had to have a place to call home, a land of their own. And to keep it in the face of repeated invasion by other wanderers they needed a strong central government and a powerful army. In the Books of Samuel and Kings we will see how this strong government came to be and at what price the people gained security in their new home.

The people of God: Already in this small near-eastern kingdom we see the primitive outlines of the Church, the people of God, whom Jesus redeemed with his own blood.

Two-sided story: We just spoke of the price the people would have to pay for a strong central government. It meant taxes, levies for armies, and on occasion, terrible despotism and corruption. The kings would frequently forget that they were merely representing God, the only ruler in Israel, and imitate the tyrannical policies of the neighboring princes. The Books of Samuel reflect these two sides of the story. The king, God's visible representative, is a sacred person, the one from whose line would one day come the looked-for Messiah. On the other hand, the king might also be a corrupt and vicious dictator who would lead the people into idolatry and the eventual misery of exile far from the land of promise.

Our task: There are many ways of approaching King David. He was a military leader, statesman, adventurer, and poet. Our approach will be that of a saint in the making. You may have to readjust your idea of sanctity. There is nothing of the plaster image about King David. Often he may remind us of a depraved king like the oriental potentates we meet in the pages of the Arabian nights, rather than the saintly composer of religious songs. But God's grace works in an infinite variety of ways. When God works with people he takes them as he finds them with all their faults and weaknesses. Their transformation shows us the marvelous power of God's grace. Who would think a young libertine like Augustine could become a shining glory of the Church? But nothing is impossible with God.

The growth of a person in holiness is often a gradual process, perhaps with many setbacks. No one is a saint until the moment of death; and if he isn't then, he never will be!

Our readings have been selected to point up the growth of David in sanctity. To trace the interplay between God's grace and a person's cooperation or resistance to it is a fascinating study.

NOW OPEN YOUR BIBLE AND READ:

FIRST BOOK OF SAMUEL
Chapters 13 through 28
SECOND BOOK OF SAMUEL
Chapter 1 through 8, and chapters 11, 12, and 22.

(NOTE: the readings suggested above give the high points in the life of David the shepherd-king. The reader may wish, however, to read more about this period in the history of God's people. Probably no other part of the Bible makes more interesting reading than the Books of Samuel and Kings. Cecil B. De Mille once said he could make a movie out of every line in these books. We strongly urge the reader not to stop with the few selections given here but to read the whole of the two books.)

behind the words

Political situation: With the close of the era of the Judges, ancient Israel faced a situation similar in many ways to the situation faced by the founders of our own country. At the close of the Revolutionary War the separate states formed a loose federation and gave no real power to the token federal government. It was seen that such a situation would not work for we were menaced by jealous European states anxious to carve a slice of the new continent for themselves, not to mention England anxious to regain her lost colonies.

The Jews had been able to manage fairly well with a loose federation when their only opponents were the petty princelings of Canaan. But with the arrival of the Philistines and their lightning invasion of the coastal area, a situation rapidly developed which called for the most drastic measures.

The Philistines: These were the natural enemies of the Israelites. Everything conspired to place them at loggerheads. Different racial origins, language, religion and civilization. In matters of warfare and culture they were superior to the Jews in every way: expert mariners, daring adventurers who had roved far and wide along the coasts of the Mediterranean. In physical stature they towered over the short, stocky sons of Israel. Their greatest hold over the tribes of Israel was their prowess as charioteers and their jealously guarded secret of metal working. They had weapons of iron. The Israelites still only had softer bronze tools and weapons. The Philistines were a formidable enemy, and it is interesting to note that it is by their name that we know the Holy Land today, Palestine.

The Philistines were great seafarers and occupied a position in the ancient world roughly equivalent to that of England during the Elizabethan period or the Norse raiders of Leif Erickson in an earlier day.

After establishing the heart of their maritime empire on the island of Crete, they attempted an invasion of Egypt during the reign of Pharaoh Rameses III (1195-1164 B.C.). Meeting with defeat, they next turned their warlike attentions to the coast of Canaan.

Here they were quite successful and gradually moved inland. During the period of the Judges they managed to establish their dominion over the Israelites who were never again to be completely free of Philistine pressure throughout the period of the Old Testament.

The Philistines disappeared from the stage of history when their country was absorbed into the Roman Province of Syria under General Pompey in the first century, B.C.

WRITE IN THE MARGIN OF YOUR BIBLE THE FOLLOWING KEY WORDS:

"Saul rejected"
— next to I SAMUEL ch.13:1
"David chosen"
— next to I SAMUEL ch.16:1
"Saul vs. David"
— next to I SAMUEL ch.18:1 and 20:42
"Saul spared"
— next to I SAMUEL ch.26:1
"Saul and the witch"
— next to I SAMUEL ch.28:3
"David mourns"
— next to II SAMUEL ch.1:17
"David dances"
— next to II SAMUEL ch.6:1
"David sins"
— next to II SAMUEL ch.11:1

"David sings"
    — next to II SAMUEL ch.22:1

understanding these selections

David chosen: (I SM. ch.16-17)   In reading the life of David the reader will notice a two-fold source for some of the events in David's career. In these chapters there are two accounts of how David was introduced to the court of Saul. In the first Saul sought a harpist, and a servant suggested David. In the second, David volunteered to fight Goliath. It seems that the historian selected from various sources in composing his book and didn't worry too much about harmonizing the various differences. The sacred author included both accounts, even though they didn't gibe in every detail, probably because both had been preserved and both were interesting. In passing it is interesting to note that the four books known as Samuel and Kings are really a single work. The division is purely an artificial one as the narrative flows right along.

David mourns: (II SM. ch.1:17-27)   David's lament for Saul and Jonathan is one of the masterpieces of ancient literature. The depth of human feeling it reflects does credit to the great heart of David. Perhaps, in a way, it throws some interesting light on the words God uses to describe the young shepherd, "A man after my own heart."

The capture of Jerusalem: (II SM. ch.5:1-16)   This marks the high point of David's career. Jerusalem was the ideal spot for the new capital as its geographic position made a perfect anchor for uniting the northern and southern factions of the kingdom. The bringing of the Ark to Jerusalem made it not only the political but the religious heart of the country as well. As the centuries passed Jerusalem was to become a sacred symbol of all that the Jews hoped for in the messianic era. It is no accident that the Church and the heavenly kingdom are spoken of as the New Jerusalem in the pages of the New Testament and the liturgy.

David's covenant: (II SM. ch.7:5-16)   The Davidic Covenant was a milestone in the history of God's plan for our redemption. Not only is the old Mosaic Covenant renewed, but now the kingship, despite its recent origin, is to share in the solidity of the Covenant. The work of Moses is completed in David, and his dynasty will now have the duty of collaborating with God in bringing his plan to the fulfillment of Christ.

David's sin: (II SM. ch.11:1 to 12:25)   The account of Nathan's confrontation of David with his sin is one of the most dramatic in all literature. From this time on David is a changed man. His life becomes embroiled in a tangle of difficulties and sorrows which are to have terrible consequences for the future of his family and the whole of Israel.

David sings: (II SM. ch.22:1-51)   David's hymn of thanksgiving which is reproduced in the Psalter as Psalm 18 has been selected to give some idea of David's poetical gifts but principally as a character portrait of the man himself. It forms a fitting conclusion to our study of the life of the Shepherd-King.

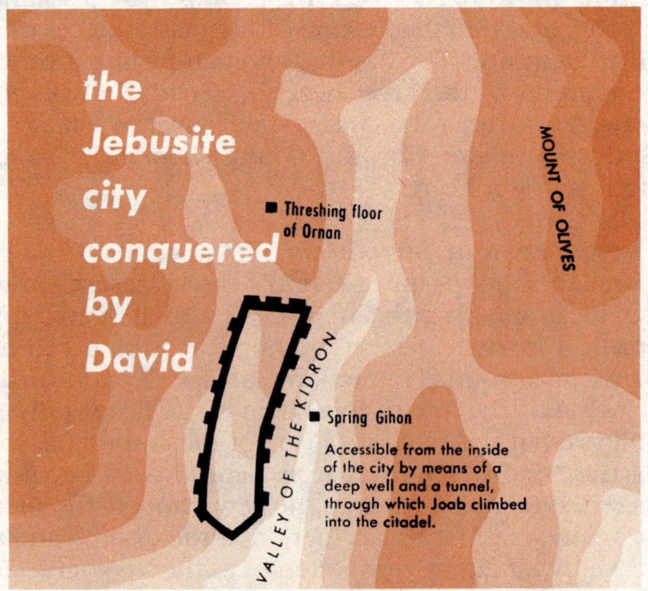

the unity of the two testaments

Son of David: Throughout the pages of the New Testament Our Lord is constantly described as the "Son of David". In spite of the many infidelities of David's descendants (described so graphically in I and II Kings) God is faithful to his promise. Jesus has come to inaugurate the kingdom of David.

But the true kingdom of Christ is very different from the earthly kingdom of David. As he said to Pontius Pilate, "My kingdom is not of this world" JOHN ch.18:36. The full manifestation of Christ's kingdom will come only at the end of time.

Meanwhile, the Church and each Christian is dedicated to the building up of that kingdom. It is our hope and prayer, "Thy kingdom come!" St. Paul points this out clearly in his sermon to the Jews in the synagogue at Antioch (ACTS ch.13:16-42) and St. John gives eloquent voice to the Christian's hope in the closing prayer of the last book of the Bible (APOCALYPSE ch.22:16-21).

bible and church

David more than Saul united the Israelites into one strong nation. His efforts to achieve unity and security led to a centralization of government. A strong central government has many advantages, not the least of which is a spirit of national unity and loyalty rather than a narrow tribal loyalty. But it can also lead to a cumbersome bureaucracy, isolation from other peoples, and dictatorship.

Very early the various Churches founded by the Apostles and the first evangelists recognized the need for a central authority, that of Rome. Throughout the ages the popes have been like the kings of Israel, many of them deserving the compliment Yahweh paid David when he called him "a man after my own heart". Others, however, have walked in the pathos of some of the less desirable kings of Israel.

National and individual pride, greed and materialism, insensitive and tyrannical use of authority have in the past broken the unity of the Church just as they destroyed the unity of Israel. Fortunately, from reading the history of Israel we know that God can use the sins and failings of his people to bring about a greater good.

In the decisions of Vatican Council II we can see the Spirit of God at work trying to bring his people back into some sort of unity. In the decree on Christian Unity the Church acknowledged that it made mistakes in the past which contributed to the Eastern Schism and the Protestant Reformation, and that it has something to learn from the Orthodox and the Protestants.

The effort to bring the Churches into unity will be long and slow. There will be setbacks, misunderstandings and failures. Hopefully, Catholics, Protestants, and Orthodox will have profited by their centuries of experience and learned from their mistakes that unity, respect and charity rather than sectarianism are signs of God's kingdom at work in the world.

doers of the word

David's beautiful prayer of thanksgiving made toward the end of his life is found in chapter 22 of II Samuel and in Psalm 18. Read it often to make your own key phrases from it. Read it slowly and reflectively. Put yourself in David's shoes. Get in touch with the feelings he had in the various dangers which threatened him and with his feeling of gratitude. Recall times when you faced trials and difficulties, some similar to David's, some different. Get in touch with the feelings you had at the time and with your feelings now. Then thank God in your own words.

questions

1. To what period in American history is the time of Saul and David similar?

   Why?

70

2. What reasons could you give for opposing Israel's having a king if you had lived in those times?

____

____

3. What great lesson stands out in the religious development of King David?

____

4. Give three reasons why the Philistines were able to dominate the Israelites:

a. _______________________________________

b. _______________________________________

c. _______________________________________

5. What new element was added to God's plan for our eternal happiness by the covenant made with David?

____

topics for discussion

1. What do you think of King David? How would you describe him? What are his strong and weak points?

2. Why was Saul rejected by God?

3. How would you compare Saul and David?

4. What do you think of God's treatment of David after his sin with Bathsheba?

5. If you were to write a prayer of thanksgiving, what events from your life would you include? Why?

MOVING ON

The history of God's People moves along with story after story of how different people respond to God. David, for example, is found among the sheep and becomes a shepherd-king. He has the mind and heart of Yahweh, a spirit of love evidenced in his friendship with Jonathan (I SAM. 18), in his respect for Saul even when menaced by him (I SAM. 24 & 26), and in his lament for Saul and Jonathan (II SAM. 1). Even when his loving leads him astray with Bathsheba, he is confident of God's loving forgiveness (II SAM. 12).

Unity among the twelve tribes is accomplished briefly under the leadership of this loving king, but the seeds of dissension have been sown. David's sexual passion is repeated in his son Ammon (II SAM. 13). This leads to Absalom's revenge, exile and continuous rebellion despite his father's never-failing love and patient kindness (II SAM. 13-19). The hero-king is still human and in his pride calls for a census of his people which leads to more suffering (II SAM. 24). His last days are plagued by the political aspirations of another son, Adonijah, so that he hands the kingdom over to Solomon. Solomon is heralded for his wisdom, but this talent, too, can lead to trouble. He appoints twelve administrators for the kingdom (I KINGS 5). Creeping bureaucracy leads to increased expenditures. He builds a glorious temple to Yahweh and a larger more magnificent palace for himself. Costs increase (I KGS. 7). He cleverly marries the daughters of the neighboring kings to solidify alliances, but this means more palaces, and sadly, also pagan temples. The tax burden becomes unbearable (I KGS. 11). Even a wise man's pride can be assailed. The Queen of Sheba comes with flattery and gifts and leaves with more than she has brought (I KGS.10.)

Despite all of Solomon's "wise" efforts, there are still foreign enemies threatening; even worse excessive taxation has bred discontent within the kingdom. A revolt is led by Jeroboam. It is put down and the leader runs away, only to wait in Egypt until Solomon is succeeded by his son, Rehoboam, a spoiled teen-ager who is advised by his elders to ease up on taxes. The new king prefers the advice of his party-loving companions and gives the people "a harsh answer" (I KGS. 12). The ten northern tribes, whose union with the two southern ones has been precarious since the time of David, declare their independence and accept Jeroboam as their king.

This political division resulted in a religious separation as well. The northern tribes set up two sanctuaries in the north to rival the temple at Jerusalem. The rest of the story of the kings of Israel and Juda is one of increasing alienation and terrible disintegration. But Yahweh again will work through this for the benefit of his people. While the externals of political and religious unity fall apart, the people will be brought eventually to discover the inner spiritual kingdom and unity God desires for them. They will look for another shepherd-king, a son of David, who will not be just physically impressive like Saul, not just intellectually gifted like Solomon, but who will balance his talents of mind and body with the spirit of love. They will hope for a king like David, a wise ruler, a strong soldier, a prayerful man, and a man of compassion and love.

This was the ideal image of a future savior that the prophets began to develop as they continued to call the people to repent and to believe in God's plan of salvation. But how easy it was to emphasize one part of the picture and to ignore another; how difficult it was for the people to harmonize *the* Isaiah's picture of a Suffering Servant with that of a powerful king and savior. The challenge of every age has been to see the whole picture and to strive to imitate the ideal of balanced humanity. Even those who have seen it fleshed out in Jesus of Nazareth are tempted to look and listen with narrowed vision and limited hearing.

LESSON 7

Assyrian archer

The Prophet . . . A People's Conscience

"The LORD GOD speaks—who will not prophesy!"
AMOS ch.3:8

BEFORE YOU OPEN YOUR BIBLE

NOTE: Several hundred years have elapsed between the reign of King David and the days of Amos the prophet. The history of this period is recorded in I and II Kings.

Brother against brother: The struggle for control between David and Saul finally resulted in secession of the ten northern tribes after the reign of Solomon, David's son. The northern tribes, always favorable to Saul, revolted and succeeded in establishing a separate kingdom called Israel (or Samaria). The tiny remnant of David's kingdom was called Juda.

God's spokesman: Although the People of God were straying ever farther from fidelity to their Covenant, God did not abandon them. Throughout the whole period of the monarchy and even during the later exile, God made known his will through the prophets.

Our task: Amos is often represented as the Karl Marx of the Old Testament. But his opposition to the wealthy is not based only upon their oppression of the poor (this was a mere symptom) but rather upon their

75

corrosive pride which was the real cause of the final destruction of both Israel and Juda. It will be our task to discover the workings of this pride as it is expressed in the words of the prophet.

NOW OPEN YOUR BIBLE AND READ:

BOOK OF AMOS
Chapters 3 through 6 and
Chapters 7:10 through 9:15

NOTE: We are omitting the first two chapters, as they have many allusions to the recent history of Israel, familiar to the people of Amos' day but now largely obscured by the passage of time. One point of interest they have for the modern reader is that they were probably an oratorical trick used by Amos to gather a crowd. People would always rally round to hear their enemies condemned, and once he had caught their ear, the prophet could then tell them what was really on his mind, as he does in chapters 3 to 6. However, as chapters 1 and 2 are carefully composed, and a magnificent example of prophetic oratory, you may want to read them on your own.

behind the words

The Assyrians: A new enemy had arisen to threaten the now divided kingdom. The Assyrians, the Nazis of their day, were in the midst of a rapid conquest of all the Near East. Their method was the ancient equivalent of the blitzkrieg. Wherever they went terror spread before them and was their strongest ally. Israel, head buried in the sand, was about to become the victim of another Assyrian conquest.

Religion in the north: To preserve their political independence the kings of the new state of Israel severed all religious ties with Juda as well. People were not permitted to go on pilgrimage to the Temple at Jerusalem, and native Northern shrines to Yahweh were established at Bethel and Dan. The Northern brand of Yahwehism grew more and more idolatrous as the years passed, adopting many of the licentious customs of the old Canaanite fertility cults.

Civilization in the north: Because of its location, Samaria was much more accessible to the great centers of commerce and culture than little, mountainous Juda. During the years of separation the northern kingdom grew very wealthy. But as often happens the rich grew richer and the poor poorer. In fact the poor were reduced to virtual slavery.

Amos the man: Amos was probably a migratory worker. During the harvest seasons he trimmed the sycamore trees in the coastal region. The rest of the year he would hire out as a drover. He was uneducated, but deeply read in the book of nature. Though humble in origin, he had the countryman's ability to speak his mind in plain language, and although a stranger to the North and of little importance in the eyes of the wealthy of Samaria, he carried out his mission with force. Grace combined with his naturally forceful character made him a person to be reckoned with in the ivory palaces of Israel.

WRITE IN THE MARGIN OF YOUR BIBLE THE FOLLOWING KEY WORDS:

> "Prologue"
> — next to AMOS ch.1-2
> "Oracles against Israel"
> — next to AMOS ch.3-6
> "Five Visions"
> — next to AMOS ch.7-9:10
> "Epilogue"
> — next to AMOS ch.9:11-15

understanding these selections

A "chosen people":   (AM. ch.3:1-2) The term "chosen people" had come in Amos' day to be a source of great pride and complacency for the Israelites. They felt because God had chosen them through

Abraham that he had to make good on his promises regardless of their conduct. How different a meaning the prophet gives to the idea of being chosen!

The "remnant": (AM. ch.3:13-4:5) In this line Amos touches on an important theme in the prophetic writings, the "remnant". Although God's people had been false to his covenant and would be severely punished, a few would be spared and would be the beneficiaries of the promises.

The great condemnation: (AM. ch.3:13-4:5) Here Amos begins his great condemnation of the callous-hearted rich and their false piety. Certainly no social reformer's words ever burned with a brighter fire of indignation.

"Yet you returned not to me": (AM. ch.4:6-11) Harsh though his words may be, there is no vindictiveness here. Only the tortured cry of a rejected lover. God sees his people abandoning him for the road which leads to death and destruction, and despite his pleading "they will not return."

"The "day of the Lord": (AM. ch.5:18-27) This passage is a magnificent portrait of the grandeur of God and his infinite power and majesty. This is contrasted sharply with the rebellion of little man and the consequent day of judgment. This "day of the Lord" was a popular idea with the children of Israel. It was to be the day of their triumph over the nations. How different is the picture of this "day" which the prophet paints. Here, too, we find an eloquent plea for the paramount importance of interior religion.

the unity of the two testaments

In Amos ch.3:12 we are told of a "remnant" of Israel which will be restored. St. Paul takes up this same theme in his letter to the Romans, ch.11.

God will not completely abandon his people. For, though man is faithless, God is faithful. The prophets hold out a hope of restoration. This hope was fulfilled when a small band of exiles returned under the Persian Empire at the close of the 6th Century B.C. This band of returned exiles was a foreshadowing of the even smaller remnant of God's chosen people who would one day greet the coming of his Son.

bible and church

Unity among God's people is achieved slowly and through much effort, but lost so quickly and easily when pride and selfishness are stronger than humility and generosity. The kings of Israel were supposed to lead their people to God and to be the visible sign of the unity of the kingdom. They were supposed to be models of faithfulness to Yahweh, but most of them ended up reflecting in their lives the sinfulness of their people. They led their people away from the worship of the true God and caused divisions among them.

In the failure of the external sign of kingship to bring the Israelites to God we can discover our need as a Church to develop and strengthen the internals. Prophets appear on the scene to insist that we search our souls. We become so dependent on that which is superficial that we find it hard to listen to their message. It is so much easier to rationalize injustice than to remedy it; so much more reassuring to idolize the non-essentials in religious practice than to make the effort to apply the essential commandment of love; so much more comforting to be complacent about all we have done in the past than to work for a future harvest.

The prophets of our day are those who call the Church to work for justice and charity, for peace, for disarmament, for freeing the oppressed, for a revision of the social and economic order. They may be even less polished than Amos. They may be less tactful than we would like them to be, but their voices must be given a hearing if the Church is to be true to its calling.

We can, as most of the Israelites did, ignore the voices of the prophets. We can try to silence them, even imprison or kill them, but in the long run they will be seen as the ones speaking for God.

doers of the word

The Pope and bishops have, in the last century, condemned the economic abuses of both capitalism and communism. They have not used the fiery language of Amos, but they have spoken as clearly and decisively. When these encyclicals and pastoral letters are released, we face the same choices the Israelites faced when Amos spoke.

We can close our ears to them and ignore them totally. We can be content with the status quo and refuse to hear anyone challenge it.

We can hear our leaders, but challenge their right to speak on economic and social matters. We can say that they should stick to preaching religion and go on acting and thinking as we always have.

Or we can listen to them and enter into a serious discussion of the problems and suggested solutions. In their latest letters the bishops have asked for this type of discussion. By reading and discussing these teachings we gradually begin to look at our ideas and actions in the light of the Gospels and of Catholic teaching.

questions

1. What is the basic reason for Amos' terrible condemnation of Israel?

____

____

2. What are two specific injustices Amos condemned?

a. _____________________________

b. _____________________________

3. Give two texts from Amos which hold out a promise of hope for ultimate salvation.

a. _____________________________

b. _______________________________________

4. Who was the new enemy which the men of Amos'
   day faced and who was to be the instrument of
   God's judgment upon Israel and Juda?

   ____

5. What different meaning does Amos give to the
   phrases "Chosen People" and "Day of the Lord"
   from what his fellow Jews understood by them?

   a. _______________________________________

   b. _______________________________________

topics for discussion

1. Why would you or would you not select a man like
   Amos for such an important mission?

2. What are some modern situations similar to those
   condemned by Amos?

3. In light of Amos' preaching what would you say to
   someone who said that the clergy should stick to
   religion and not speak out on economic and social
   problems?

4. In light of Amos' idea of religion expressed in
   chapter 5:21-24 what would you see as the most
   important task of the Church?

BACKGROUND:

God Speaks in Many Ways

To understand and appreciate the Bible, you must find out exactly what the authors are trying to say. This is not so easy as one might think. For, behind the words on the printed page, lie a great many questions which you must answer if you would be sure of getting the meaning the author intended. For instance, from what point of view is he treating his subject? How is he presenting his material? As a simple factual account? An opinion? An obvious untruth which he certainly rejects along with us? Is the statement he seems to make actually proposed by the author, or is it something we are reading into his words? Does the author expect us to take him literally in this or that passage?

Scholars who deal with these perplexing problems find a great deal of help in reaching a solution by studying the particular literary form which the author adopted for his work. Depending upon whether he is going to teach, or inspire, or prove, or convince, or entertain, or pray, the author will select the most suitable form of literature.

Modern authors do much the same thing. A thought or idea may be expressed in a novel, a play, an essay, a poem, or a technical work depending upon the author's purpose.

For example, you know that historical novels, poems, newspaper accounts, and text books require a different mind set when you read them. When you pick up a book you instinctively "adjust your sights" to the literary form the author is using.

The same is true when you take up the Bible. There are many different kinds of literature in it. Book differs from book. In the same book, two or three different literary forms may be used.

Different times and different cultures produce different types of literature. In the Bible there are literary forms we no longer use. Bible forms which appear to be the same as those we use, may be different in significant aspects.

Hebrew historical writing and modern history books are similar but by no means the same in the way they report the events of the past. And this different approach does not necessarily make one true and the other false. Each has its own contribution to make to our understanding of the "whole truth."

We have already seen some examples of different kinds of literary forms in the preceding lessons. In the story of Abraham we met a sample of "family history" or "folk chronicle." We have seen how the Jews wrote law in Exodus and Deuteronomy. In the Book of Joshua we sampled a kind of historical writing, which flowed in broad strokes, and might almost be called a kind of "theology of history," while in Judges we found a collection of traditional biographies of great popular heroes of Israel's past.

In the Books of Samuel and Kings we came across still another variety of historical writing. This time we found what might be considered the closest ancient equivalent to what we imagine historical writing ought to be.

In these last lessons we meet still two more special kinds of writing. In lesson seven we saw a prophetical oratory and in lesson eight we will examine that very special little literary gem, a wonderful wedding of poetic imagery, deep human insight, and divine truth, the Creation account in Genesis.

Each of these various kinds of literature calls for a different "mind set" on the part of the reader, if he would understand the writing on its own terms. We have tried to point out in these notes something of the approach or "mind set" you should have for reading each of these books.

The literary form, then, is the envelope of God's message to men. The form may differ depending upon who the human collaborator may have been. It may be beautiful or ugly depending upon the native literary genius of the human author. But since God has deigned to take human beings into partnership, he takes them with their literary shortcomings as well as their literary talents.

LESSON 8

"in the beginning . . ." GENESIS *1:1*

The Meaning of Creation

BEFORE YOU OPEN YOUR BIBLE

God's story of creation: We now take up what is, without doubt, one of the great religious statements of all time. In twelve short chapters of the Book of Genesis we find one of the most sublime descriptions of the very heart and soul of religion. The portrait of God sketched in Genesis encompases his infinite majesty and his tender concern for humankind. The human race is presented in all its dignity and glory as well as in its inherent and inherited weaknesses. But these chapters are not merely a statement of the religious facts of life, they are also a ringing appeal to Adam and Eve's descendants to live up to their great vocation of being God's image and likeness!

Why read the creation story at this point? It may seem strange to wait until the People of God are on the threshold of exile from the promised land before taking up the story of the creation of the world. But the reason we have waited so long is that the account, as we have it in the first twelve chapters of the Book of Genesis, is told to us in a very special way. If you don't know the people who speak to you, if you have no idea of their customs, their way of looking at things, you may easily misunderstand what they are telling you. For this reason you have first become acquainted with the little tribe of Abraham before sitting down to listen to their explanation of some of the basic questions of life.

How was the creation story put together?   The first eleven chapters of the Book of Genesis have a long, long history. It is really a little book in itself and took about twelve hundred years to reach its present form! Some of the elements of the account go back many centuries before the time of Abraham. It was first written down around the 8th century B.C. Its principal elements had formed the content of the stories told around the campfires of the wandering tribe of Abraham for centuries before that time. Many of the images and expressions used are taken from the common folklore of the people of the Middle East. Remember, the authors were men of their times and so were their hearers, and naturally thought and wrote in the imagery of the ancient East. Of course, they stripped this imagery of all its pagan trappings.

What is the Genesis story?   We might call it an argument cast in poetic and imaginative language. The authors say to the pagan world around them, "You are wrong! The world is not an accident, but the carefully planned work of the one true God!" It was composed to set the people of God straight on the basic religious questions of life. The authors are very anxious to arm their people against the fantastic explanations of the origin of the human race and the universe which were current among their pagan neighbors.

Some pagans thought the world and human beings were an accident, a mere by-product of a war among the gods. Others looked upon the material world as the creation of an evil god, while the world of spirit was the handiwork of a good god. Human beings, then, were pitiful creatures, spirits imprisoned in flesh!

In contrast to these various explanations, a hodge-podge of fantasy and even vulgarity, the account of Genesis stands apart in its sublimity, beauty and elevated tone.

NOW OPEN YOUR BIBLE AND READ:

BOOK OF GENESIS
Chapters 1 through 11

behind the words

Was the world created the way the author of Genesis describes the Creation?

No, God through collaboration with the human author was trying to put across in a simple, easily understood way the basic truths of man's destiny and purpose in life. His audience was a primitive, simple group of nomads. For this reason he described things to them in a non-scientific way. They had no telescopes or microscopes, they only had their eyes. He described things the way they appeared to people's perceptions.

Is the story of Genesis a true story?

Yes, if we take the author on his own terms. To understand what the author is trying to tell us we must put out of our minds such questions as, "Did God really create the world in seven periods of 24 hours each?" "Was there a real tree, and what kind of fruit did our first parents eat?" We must approach the account in a truly scientific manner and ask the proper questions, "What is the message of Genesis? What great answers are offered here by God to the questions which have puzzled mankind for centuries?"

What is the message of Genesis?

God who had made man and woman, knew the questionings of their hearts. Loving them with an everlasting love, he entrusted to one people, as guardians of the truth, some of the basic answers so that they might not grope in darkness forever.

a. There is only one God and everything depends upon him. Even the great sun and moon, so awe-inspiring that many men had turned to them in worship, were God's handiwork.

b. God is all-powerful and the author brings this out by describing the act of creation as a mere word of command, "God spoke and it was so!"

c. God is a God of order and harmony, so like a true craftsman the author describes him as going about the work of creation in much the same fashion as a skilled carpenter will build a house. He chose to describe creation as if taking place in a single week in order to point up God's great power and orderly plan, even though scientifically speaking the work of creation may have taken millions of years.

d. To crown His work God made man and woman. Though they are one of the smallest of God's creatures, they are one of the most important, for God had given them the awesome task of ruling over and subduing all the rest of God's handiwork. In short, they were made in God's image and likeness because like God, who rules the universe, they were to exercise dominion over the world.

WRITE IN THE MARGIN OF YOUR BIBLE THE FOLLOWING KEY WORDS:

"God prepares a home for the human race"
— next to GENESIS ch.1:1, 2:3
"The creation and fall of the first man and woman"
— next to GENESIS ch.2:4, 3:6
"The effects of Adam's sin"
— next to GENESIS ch.3:7

understanding these selections

"God prepares a home for the human race": (GN. ch.1:-2:3) In reading the Creation story, we must always keep in mind that the authors of Genesis were not philosophers. Abstract ideas like "nothingness" had no meaning for them. The closest they could come to an idea of "creation", i.e., the production of something where nothing had existed before, was to describe it as a putting of order into a vast chaos. In other words they expressed their ideas in a concrete way. The philosopher has given an exactness and clarity to those ideas. The explanations of creation we find in our catechisms benefit from the labors of the philosophers, but we should try to read Genesis in the way it was written and not quarrel with the authors if they are not familiar with the refinements of philosophy.

Again and again in the pages of Genesis we read "and God saw that it was good". (GN ch.1:4) The authors wanted their hearers to clearly understand that everything was created by the one God who is all good and who shares his goodness with his creation. Nothing that God has made is bad in itself. This depends upon how people exercise their dominion over it.

The ordering of the work of creation within the framework of a week (GN. ch.1:5), was done to show us that creation was not an accident but a carefully planned procedure, and also to give a religious significance to the Sabbath rest.

Far from being gods themselves, the authors show how God has placed the stars and the sun and moon in the heavens to serve people, acting as aids to navigation and providing light and warmth for them. (GN. ch.1:14).

The creation and fall of the first man and woman: (GN. ch.1:27-2:18-25) Here, the authors present their sublime teaching on sex. They show how people's reproductive function is a blessing from God. They go on later (GN. ch.2:18-25) to describe how man and woman are equal in dignity (woman comes from man and is his helpmate), that woman completes man ("it is not good for man to be alone"), and in marriage they find perfect and unbreakable union (two in one flesh).

The effects of Adam's sin: (GN. ch.3:1-ch.11:19) Unlike the rest of his creatures God has given to men and women the wonderful privilege of offering him a free service of love. But this privilege carried with it the possibility of refusal to serve and the loss of God's special gift of supernatural life. Here (GN. 3:1-9), the author explains the fall of the human race in a way

which takes into account that vague feeling in everyone's heart that there was once some terrible calamity
that altered the course of history and brought in its
wake suffering and death. The psychological process
of temptation outlined here is a masterpiece of sensi-
tive and acute observation of human nature. Note the
various steps:

a. the tempter sows a doubt about God's goodness.
   (ch.3:1)

b. the woman dallies with temptation instead of dis-
   missing it. (ch.3:2)

c. the serpent implies God is mean and jealous of his
   position. (ch.3:4-5)

d. he further holds out as bait a new experience.
   (ch.3:5)

e. the final step where the woman takes over and the
   seed sown by the devil blossoms into sin. (ch.3:6)

Now in a masterful series of episodes, the authors
describe the terrible consequences of using one's
dominion against God, and how it blows up in one's
face.

a. Adam and Eve lose their perfect control over themselves and discover a conflict of desires and emo-
   tions within themselves, giving rise to shame. (GN.
   ch.3:7)

b. The perfect *harmony* between *man and wife* is
   disrupted and turned into bickering and blame-
   shifting. (GN. ch.3:12-13)

c. Adam and Eve find that they have lost their *effort-
   less dominion* over the world about them. They
   now find nature "red in tooth and claw". But in
   his words to the serpent, God shows he has not
   abandoned them, but hold out to them the *promise
   of restoration.* (GN. ch.3:13-19)

d. *Death* is now their fate and is an image of the loss
   of that eternal life which God had originally intended for all people. (GN. ch.3:19)

e. Following close upon the fall, comes a second sin,
   the *first murder.* (GN. 4:1-16) The authors' first

readers, being desert wanderers, were quite familiar with the constant struggle and rivalry between the rootless nomads and the settled farmers. It was natural then, for the authors to describe the "bad guy", Cain, as a "tiller of the soil."

f. In the story of *the flood* (GN. 6:5-9:17), we are shown to what depths of sin and degradation Adam's descendants had sunk. Scholars tell us that the way in which the authors depict the terrible calamity does not necessarily mean that the deluge was worldwide. But the letter of the text is quite satisfied if we suppose an extensive flooding of the valley of the Tigris and Euphrates, which was certainly the "whole world" for the people of that time and place.

   Archeologists have shed much light on the flood story in recent years. They have discovered large layers of clay and sediment in the plain of the Tigris and Euphrates Valley. In digging they find layer upon layer of remains of ancient civilizations. Often they will then come across a layer of mud and clay extending down for many feet, indicating a serious flood which wiped out all signs of civilization for many years. Finally, they will break through the clay and once more begin to find relics of the ancient past.

   Such floods seem to have been more or less common in this region, which has been called the "cradle of civilization". These floods which from time to time, wrought such havoc, would seem to form the background for our story of the Great Flood.

g. The covenant with Noah (GN. ch.9:9-17) is important in that it shows that the God of the Jews is the Father of all people. The whole human race has a part to play in this covenant, and will share the eventual benefits of God's plan.

h. Here again, in the story of the *Tower of Babel,* (GN. ch.11:1-9) we find people attempting to exercise their "dominion" apart from God—original sin repeating its dismal story. As background to the story

of the Tower of Babel imagine, if you will, the long
lasting impression which the great commercial and
trading centers of Babylon made on the little bands
of nomads passing along its fringes. From time to
time they would enter the great cities bringing a
shipment of desert products for trading in its great
bazaars. The high temple platforms, looking like artificial mountains, erected by the Babylonians to
their gods could be seen reflecting golden rays of
the setting sun from the small bedouin en-
campments where the Hebrew traders would retire
after a long day of haggling in the market place. A
thread of suspicion and enmity, felt by these simple
desert people for these great citadels of power and
idolatry, runs through the story of Babel.

the unity of the two testaments

The new Adam: The writers of the New Testament
saw in our Lord the "new Adam." St. Paul best sums it
up in the fifth chapter of his letter to the Romans,
verses 12 to 21.

The new creation: "What we await are new
heavens and a new earth where, according to his
promise, the justice of God will reside." (2 PETER
ch.3:13). This "new heaven and new earth" is the
restoration of people to God through Christ and his
Church. This new work of creation is still being carried forward. It will not reach its completion until the
last day. Still, the major part is already completed in
Christ's life and work. (ROMANS ch.8:18-25). It is Christ
who unites both Jews and Gentiles in his death and
makes of them a single "new man"—the Church,
which is the new humanity. (I CORINTHIANS
ch.12:12-14).

To see how deeply the Gospel writers appreciated
Christ as the New Adam, and the work of Redemption
as a new creation in Grace, we need only to turn to the
prologue of the Gospel of St. John. There we find that
the Evangelist deliberately parallels the very words of
the first chapter of Genesis!

bible and church

Today on all sides we hear a call for renewal in the Church. There are all kinds of renewal programs available. But programs alone will not renew a parish or a diocese. A time of renewal is a time of reorganization with a new or rediscovered vision. One element of this vision is hope, the unfaltering trust that God has something wonderful in store for his people in spite of all their failings.

The Scriptures radiate this hope. When the Israelites returned from exile and began to rebuild their temple and country, they gathered the stories of their people that spoke not only of how it was but also of how it could be. Even in the negative incidents of their past they saw a positive message calling them to dream of what a loving and caring Yahweh wanted for them.

The very first story in the Bible is, on the surface, a terrible tragedy. Adam and Eve had been created in the image and likeness of God. He had empowered them to cultivate the garden with goodness and to do battle against those who would destroy it. Instead they had tried to reach beyond what they were and

93

become like God himself. Their pride and selfishness had ruined the beauty and harmony God intended them to have. But God gave them hope that one day a savior would come.

When Jesus the Christ did come, he gave us brief glimpses of the Paradise to be. He met and overcame the tempter in the desert; it became a garden in which angels and beasts waited upon him. The Garden of Gethsemane was transformed by his obedience from a place of sorrow to a place where people and God were once again in harmony. The sufferings of Calvary proved the power of love to change a burial ground into a garden of resurrection.

Jesus gives us a vision of what will be as he plants and replants the seed of life through the renewal efforts of his Church. We as Church are called to work toward this fulfillment with all our God-given talents and power.

doers of the word

The story of creation makes it very clear that God has placed the care of this planet in our hands. We are to care for its resources. We are to care for its birds, fish, animals and plants. We are to use its resources wisely and prudently for the benefit of all, especially those of future generations.

This responsibility has become much heavier in the last few years. The population explosion and the need for more land is threatening the rain forests of the Amazon which play an important role in the earth's weather. The depletion of the earth's resources of coal, oil, timber will have a great impact on future generations.

In the Book of Genesis we see what happens when we do not use God's gifts wisely. Individually we cannot do much, but we can do something. United with others we can reverse the course we are taking.

questions

1. What kind of history is the Book of Genesis?

2. What is the message of the story of creation?

a. _______________________________________

b. _______________________________________

c. _______________________________________

d. _______________________________________

3. Does the rivalry between Cain and Abel reflect another rivalry familiar to the ancient Israelites?

____

4. How does the story of the Tower of Babel express the feelings of the little tribe of Abraham towards the mighty Babylonian civilization?

____

topics for discussion

1. We all ask basic questions about ourselves, about God, and about the world around us. Make a list of these questions for yourself and of the answers the Book of Genesis gives.

2. Discuss how the psychological process of temptation outlined in Genesis operates in various ways in daily life.

3. In what way do you think we are made in the image and likeness of God? What are the consequences of this likeness in our daily lives?

4. There are two basic views of human nature after the fall. One sees us as fallen and essentially corrupt and sinful. The other sees us as fallen but still basically good. Which of these theories is closest to what you believe? Why?

QUESTIONS OF CHRISTIANS:

Explores the answers of the writers of the New Testament to the questions that the early believers must have asked. This program includes audio cassettes as well as discussion questions and commentary on the Gospels.

Vol. 1 **Mark's Response**
Vol. 2 **Matthew's Response**
Vol. 3 **Luke's Response**
(Other volumes in preparation)

SCRIPTURE DISCUSSION COMMENTARIES:

Short, easy to read, modern commentaries on the entire Bible. Designed to promote discussion. Available in single volumes, or as a complete set of 12 books.

1. **Pentateuch:** Genesis, Exodus, Deuteronomy—**256 pgs**
2. **Prophets I:** Amos, Hosea, Isaiah, Jeremiah—**244 pgs**
3. **Histories I:** Judges, Ruth, 1 and 2 Samuel, 1 and 2 Kings—**192 pgs**
4. **Prophets II:** Ezekial, Daniel, Minor Prophets—**192 pgs**
5. **Histories II:** Joshua, 1 and 2 Chronicles, Ezra, Nehemiah, 1 and 2 Maccabees—**224 pgs**
6. **Wisdom:** Psalms, Job, Wisdom, Proverbs, Ecclesiastes, Sirach—**256 pgs**
7. **Mark and Matthew:** Gospels—**256 pgs**
8. **Luke:** Gospel, Acts, 1 Peter—**192 pgs**
9. **John:** Gospel, Epistles, 1, 2, and 3 James—**256 pgs**
10. **Paul I:** Galatians, Romans, Ephesians, 1 and 2 Thessalonians—**224 pgs**
11. **Paul II:** 1 and 2 Corinthians, Phililppians, Colossians, Philemon—**224 pgs**
12. **Last Writings:** Hebrews, Pastoral Epistles, Revelation, 2 Peter—**92 pgs**